Foreword

I know, from my own personal experie[...] book will be for parents who are overw[...] suffering over the death of their baby. [...] [...]...ons of joyful anticipation have been turned, in an instant, into a time of despairing loss and emptiness, with long months ahead struggling to regain a normal world once more.

Some of these feelings are of isolation and dealing with inexplicable and frightening emotions which no-one else can understand. This book will undoubtedly bring comfort and support to parents who are caught in this agonising situation, and to their families and friends who so often feel powerless to help.

Reading the very sensitive stories of other bereaved parents is a real help in dealing with feelings of isolation and not being able to explain or even understand - some of one's own reactions. The book is also very helpful in explaining how other parents have found different ways of being able to express their grief and find comfort.

I am sure bereaved parents caught in the frighteningly fierce storm of their emotions will be helped to find a way back eventually to peace and calm, while still keeping a few treasured memories.

Patricia Mountbatten of Burma

Countess Mountbatten of Burma
CBE, CD, JP, DL

Countess Mountbatten of Burma is the mother of seven children including identical twin sons (the youngest). At the age of 14 the eldest twin, Nicholas, was killed with his grandfather, Earl Mountbatten of Burma (and his grandmother, Doreen Brabourne) when the IRA blew up his small fishing boat in Ireland in 1979. She now has nine grandchildren, since the death of 5 year old Leonora from cancer.

Lady Mountbatten is married to the film and television producer Lord Brabourne, and is Vice Lord-Lieutenant of Kent and a Magistrate. She is Vice President of the British Red Cross and NSPCC and is connected to over 50 other charitable organisations.

Contents

GRIEVING
after the death of your baby

About this book

 Grieving means feeling all the sadness and the sorrow, all the anger, guilt and pain that loss can bring, and it also means doing something with those feelings. This book is about what it feels like to grieve. It is also about expressing grief.

Many of the feelings that are described in the book are feelings that people grieving for all kinds of different reasons will recognise. But this book is about one particular experience of grief - the grief that follows the loss of a baby.

Grieving is never easy, but grieving for a baby can be especially hard. The death of a baby is so shocking. It's a death that should never happen. There seems no reason why a baby should die, and for many parents, no reason is discovered for their baby's death. As a result, parents often blame themselves. They feel they have failed their baby and failed as parents. They feel angry with themselves, with doctors and nurses, with God. They feel bitter, because others have children and they have not. Above all, they feel desolation and despair because the baby they wanted has died, because their future together has been denied them, and because their love for their child now has no course to run.

Other people often don't understand. People who have little experience of loss sometimes think that, since there is less to remember when a baby dies, there must be less to grieve for - yet it is the lack of memories that makes grieving hard. They encourage parents to forget the tragedy and move on - yet no parent ever forgets. They say 'you can always have another one' - though some parents can't, and all parents know that they will never be able to replace the baby they have lost.

For all these reasons, the experience of grieving for a baby is often a very lonely one, and because they are isolated and their grief is so intense, parents often think that what they are feeling must be abnormal. Many say that they feel they are going mad with grief.

In Part One of this book, parents talk about their experience of grieving. Reading other parents' stories, although it is so sad and harrowing, is almost always reassuring. Parents talk about the relief they feel when they hear other parents' stories and realise that they are neither alone nor abnormal. Reading others' stories also puts them in touch with their own memories and feelings, and although this hurts, many say that the pain and tears are helpful.

Part Two of the book, 'Ways of Grieving', is about expressing grief. Parents and families have to find their own ways of grieving. What is helpful for one person may not be at all helpful for someone else. On the other hand, most people have very little experience of loss, and it can be hard to know what to do with feelings that are unfamiliar and sometimes frightening. 'Ways of Grieving' describes the many different ways parents have found of expressing their feelings and remembering their baby.

Part 1

STORIES ABOUT GRIEVING

These stories are taken from conversations about grief and grieving with parents and families. They talk about what happened, what they did, and how they felt in the time after their baby's death.

Grieving has been hard for all of them, but as time has passed, the pain has lessened. It's now some years since their babies died, and although they are all still grieving for the baby they loved and then lost, their grief is no longer unbearable.

Pat and Brian

Pat and Brian's daughter Holly was stillborn just before Christmas six years ago. The pregnancy had gone well but at 33 weeks, Pat became anxious that the baby wasn't moving. When she was given a scan, it showed that Holly had died. There has never been any explanation for Holly's unexpected death.

Pat It was so hard leaving the hospital. I wanted to go back to be near Holly. I felt desolate. I felt as though I'd been pushed into a dark room where I couldn't see anything and couldn't hear anything. It was as though a big iron door had been slammed shut in front of me.

After the initial shock and numbness, I had so many different feelings. You wouldn't think you could feel so much all at once. I felt angry - angry with myself, with the doctors, with Brian . . . I even felt angry at Holly for dying and leaving us feeling like this. I felt incredibly sad, very weepy. I felt confused, frustrated. There were so many intense feelings.

I felt such a failure. I felt that I'd failed as a mother, that I'd failed as a wife, and that I'd let everybody down because they were all expecting me to bring this baby home and I'd come home empty-handed.

I felt this enormous sense of guilt. The week before Holly was born, I was cleaning out the bathroom and I thought I'd give the toilet a really good clean. And I was convinced that because I'd been breathing in all these chemicals, I'd caused her death. It was irrational, but you want to know what caused it. Also, during the pregnancy, Brian and I had argued quite a lot, and at one point I'd said that I wished I wasn't pregnant. And I felt this was God's way of punishing me, by taking Holly away.

I knew that after you had a baby, your milk came through and there were all sorts of bodily changes, but I honestly thought that because our baby had died, Mother Nature would take care of that and it wouldn't happen. So when my milk came through, I was completely unprepared for it, and it just felt like a great big kick in the teeth. There was all this milk, and no baby to feed. It just felt so cruel.

It was really painful to see pregnant women. Once or twice, I had to go up to my GP's surgery, and there always seemed to be pregnant women there. When I went into town, there seemed to be hundreds and hundreds of pregnant women. It was if they were all there just to taunt me. I felt really jealous. I remember at my GP's surgery, there were pregnant women laughing and joking together, and I felt like saying to them, 'You wouldn't be laughing and joking if you'd gone through what I've gone through.' And I used to wish it on people. It sounds dreadful but it's how I felt.

I'm not the sort of person who can cry in front of people. I can talk to people about how I'm feeling, but then I have to go home and have a cry on my own. So I did my crying at night. I used to go to bed early so that I could have a good cry. I used to long to go to bed. But in the middle of the night, I'd wake up and I'd find myself reaching my arms out to hold this baby that wasn't there. I felt if I just reached my arms out, I could pull her towards me.

I felt that, because my world had stopped dead, everything else should stop too. I remember one day sitting on the top deck of a double decker bus and looking down and thinking, 'Why is everyone carrying on with their normal daily routine when this has happened? Why haven't they stopped? Why can't they feel what I'm feeling?' It didn't seem right that I should be feeling so devastated and everyone else just carrying on as normal. I felt like screaming at them, 'My baby's dead!'

About two months after Holly died, I saw a television programme about stillbirth and neonatal death, and on this programme, there were mothers talking about the feelings that they were going through. And up until then, I'd been feeling these feelings but they didn't seem normal to me. I felt as though I was going out of my mind because I'd never felt such intense feelings before. But when these mothers were describing how they felt, all of a sudden it felt okay for me, because it made me realise that what I was going through was normal and I was allowed to feel like that.

One of the things I desperately wanted was for people to acknowledge that Holly had existed. People never knew her, and a lot of people think that what you've never had, you never miss. Because we didn't get to know Holly, they thought we'd get over her death in a couple of weeks. But it doesn't work like that.

In the first two months, I would say, my every thought was Holly. I knew I was beginning to get through it and get back to some sort of normality when other thoughts would come into my head, so Holly became every other thought. Then

as each day went by, she wouldn't take up as much of my thoughts. But for the first year after she died, I felt all I was doing was saying 'This time last year . . . this time last year . . .' And it wasn't until we got to the first anniversary of her death that I felt as though I could go on and there was a future.

The first anniversary was very difficult, very painful. It just brought back all the sad memories and all the feelings that we went through at the very beginning. But now it is easier, it's not as painful, and we tend to look back at the good memories we've got. We're proud that we had her, we'll never forget her. You forget about all the really painful feelings, they're not as intense. It's getting easier as time goes by.

Brian

The first feeling I had was, 'It's not happening.' Even when my mother in law told me the news that Pat had been taken into hospital and they couldn't find the baby's heart beat, I wasn't worried. Because I felt, 'Well, they've made a mistake.' And I got to the hospital, and the sister came up to me, and she just took my hand and said, 'I'm sorry.' Those two words and that was it. It was like someone had come up and hit me with a baseball bat. I couldn't have felt any worse. I went into the room where Pat was, and even then I was half expecting her to smile at me and say, 'They're wrong.' But she shook her head and she was crying.

I think the hardest part for me at first was when people would come up to me and would say something or just squeeze my arm and say 'Are you all right?' It was the sympathy. I could cope, so long as I didn't get the sympathy. It sounds strange, but I'd be okay until someone came up to me and said, 'I'm sorry', and then the pain would all come flooding back.

I wanted to shut it out and forget everything, forget the pain and the hurt. But as soon as you do, something reminds you. Somebody says something, or you hear something on the television about babies, even the adverts . . . It's like when

you cut your finger, you seem to knock it all the time. It's the same when you've lost a baby.

At the very start, there was no way I could go to the grave with Pat. But driving past the cemetery on the way home from work, even at eleven o'clock at night, I used to pull up and I'd shine my headlights onto Holly's grave. It was as if to say, 'I haven't abandoned you, I'm still here.' And I would stand at her grave and talk away to her, just as though it was a normal conversation. But I could never tell Pat. As far as Pat was concerned, I wasn't going to the grave.

At the time, I honestly thought I was going insane. Standing by the grave, if someone had gone past and asked me what I was doing, what would I have said to them? You couldn't put it into words. You couldn't say to your best friend, 'Oh, I was down at my daughter's grave last night.' Yet the more I kept it to myself, the more I believed I was going insane. I couldn't go past the cemetery without stopping to say hello. I still feel guilty sometimes if I drive past and I don't drop in.

· I remember when I first went to the grave, I wanted to dig her up, I really did, just to see her. Because I never held her, and I feel very guilty about that. And at first, I was very, very near to digging up the grave, to hold her and say 'I'm sorry.'

I remember one day I was driving along the road, and I almost drove over to the other side. The tears were streaming down my face and I felt life wasn't worth living. For a split second, I could have quite happily gone over to the other side of the road and put an end to it. These things go through your mind.

I'm not a religious person, but I felt very, very angry with God. Pat started going to church, which she hadn't done before, and I would drive her there in the car and wait for her. The priest said to me one time, 'Why don't you come in?' And I said, 'I don't speak to your God, because your God took my daughter.' I really meant that. But he was a great priest and he understood how I felt. I would chat with him. One day, it was after our next

HOLLY

baby was born, I was sitting outside the church, and I thought, 'He's given me Callum. He's trying to make it up.' And I went inside and I sat down next to Pat in the church.'

It doesn't go away quickly. Last year, just sitting watching television, Pat was in bed, the football had finished, and I looked across at my son's nursery school photograph. The face is so like Holly's, it broke my heart. I just sat there and cried.

Pat and Brian grieved for Holly in different ways. Pat wanted to talk about Holly but Brian didn't, and for a time they drew apart.

Pat People tended to think that me and Brian would grieve together. But in actual fact, we grieved so differently and separately that we were driven apart by it for a while. I couldn't talk to Brian because the pain was too much for him. He'd look at me and it would all come back to him, what we'd

been through with the labour and the birth. If it hadn't been for my family, especially my Mum, I don't think I could have got through that early time. There was nobody else to talk to.

Brian Pat and I rowed constantly. We rowed over little things. Now we'd probably laugh about things like that, but there was no laughing in our house at that time. There was no closeness. I knew the closer I got to Pat, the more she'd want to talk about it. Pat would get so frustrated with me not wanting to speak about it, but I couldn't. I couldn't face it.

It took a year for Pat and I to go to the grave together, and I think that was the time we started to come together again. For a time we drifted apart, because she was grieving in her way, and I was grieving in mine, and it was torture, it really was, for both of us. We didn't feel for each other. Our sex life was almost non-existent. It was hard enough to even speak to each other, let alone anything else. But afterwards, when we actually realised what we were doing to each other, I think the grief brought us closer together. And I would say we were closer after that first year than we'd ever been, because we shared something, something special. It's something sad, but it's special.

In the months after Holly's death, Pat talked a lot to her mother and that helped her. But Pat's mother didn't feel that she was helping at all.

Pat In the first few weeks, my mum was probably the biggest help because she allowed me to talk about Holly. In fact, I know she was relieved when I did start talking about her. It made me realise that my mum wasn't just grieving for the granddaughter she'd lost, she was grieving for me as well. In fact, she said that she wished that she could go through it for me, to take away my pain. I think only a mother could say something like that.

We still talk about her now. Whenever I

mention Holly, we usually have a good conversation about everything that we went through and how we felt.

Pat's mother

At the time, I felt very frustrated. I wanted to help Pat but I didn't know how. How do you know how to react? You've no experience. You're not prepared for anything like this. I was watching Pat and Brian suffer all the time, and I couldn't do anything. I couldn't take the pain away, I couldn't give her the baby that she'd lost - my granddaughter.

It hurt. The pain - I couldn't believe the actual physical pain. At one time I even thought I was having a heart attack, because for a few days this pain wouldn't go, it just got worse and worse. I realise now it was grief.

I couldn't say an awful lot about how I felt to Pat, she was feeling bad enough herself. My husband was working away at the time, so I didn't have him to turn to. Most of what I felt I had to keep to myself. I used to go to bed at night and just lie there thinking. I wish I'd seen Holly. I could remember something then. There's a photograph of her, which is a bit of a comfort, but it's not like seeing her and holding her. I imagine how she might look now when I see other little girls running about who'd be the same age as Holly. But that's all. Just imagine.

At the time of Holly's death, Pat and Brian had two children - Scott, who was two years old, and Nina, who was six. Nina was looking forward to being an older sister.

Pat

My mum wanted to tell Nina for me, but I insisted on telling her myself. I didn't know how to tell her, so I decided the best thing was just to tell her the truth. I said, 'I'm sorry, Nina, but the baby's died.' I just wasn't prepared for her reaction. I thought she would be sad and cry, but instead she was really angry and she shouted at me, 'How could you let my sister die? You knew I wanted a little sister!' I thought at one point she was going to hit me. I found that really

hard to cope with. I just cuddled her, but she didn't want me, she was so angry. I was upset. Her reaction shocked me. I'd expected floods of tears, not anger. The tears came later.

Brian

The day Pat came home from hospital, she went to bed, and I went to take her a cup of tea. She was lying in bed asleep, and there in the bed beside her was a life-size doll. Nina had come in and she'd put her doll in the bed with Pat. I was shocked and really angry, and I shouted at Nina, 'What did you do that for? Are you trying to upset her?' And Nina was crying, and she said, 'No. She lost her baby, so I've given her mine.'

Kids look at it a lot better than adults. They cope better. When we went to Holly's grave a few years later, and we were taking a wreath and a card, I asked Nina to write on the card. She said, 'What shall I write?' I said, 'Just write what you want.' And Nina wrote, 'Wish you were here.'

Mohammed

Mohammed and Saleem's baby daughter Ruqiya was born early with a heart abnormality. She lived for twelve days in special care. She was their first baby, and it's now five years since she died. They have had two more daughters since Ruqiya.

They are a Moslem family, and Mohammed's faith has played an important part in his grieving.

I will always remember the day Ruqiya died. It was a very important day for me and I remember everything that happened very clearly. It was a very, very sad day for us.

I was given a lot of support. I rang and told my brothers, who live a long way away, and they were here with us the same night to try to help as much as they could. The local community also knew about it and supported us and helped us with the arrangements we had to make.

I wanted to do everything for my baby myself. One thing I wanted to do was bring her home from the hospital myself rather than get a funeral director to do it. I was able to get my own coffin made, and go to the mortuary, and pick up my daughter in my own hands, bring her to my own car and drive her home myself. That was something I very much wanted to do, and I did it.

We have a ceremonial washing of the body before the funeral, and Saleem wanted to do that. We use a particular piece of wood, that you lay the body on to wash it, and I made that myself rather than use the one in the mosque. I still have it. My mother was here, and she and Saleem

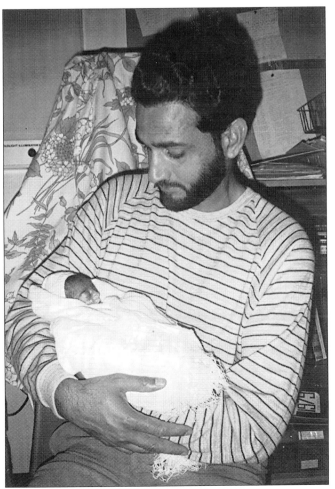

washed the baby. Then I prepared the coffin. I put all the writing on it in Arabic, and Saleem did the sewing. We did it all ourselves.

The Moslem belief is that when you die you are resurrected, and that the family will meet together, and so I believe that we will certainly see her again. We know one thing is certain, that we are all going to die. No one will live for ever. So we will meet one day, and that keeps me going.

I believe the death of Ruqiya really brought my wife and I together. Especially in the first couple of months, and even now when we look back, I can hardly believe how close we got. We didn't argue but we could sit and discuss how we could best cope. That helped us. We used to sit and talk, and sit and talk about it. We found it better to talk about things rather than isolate yourself and bottle things up inside. With emotional things, the bubble's going to burst one day, so it's better if you talk about it. We still talk about her, we still talk about our daughter.

When Saleem was expecting our next baby, obviously we were apprehensive. The doctors said that it was possible that we could have the same problem again, but we carried on, and when our next daughter was born and she was completely normal, I was over the moon and so was Saleem. But at the same time, it brought back memories of our eldest daughter. We thought about how old she would have been and what it would have been like if she was with us.

We are still grieving for Ruqiya. I don't think grieving ever stops for parents. It never ever stops. Every year, we have a special day for my daughter like we do for all the dead people. And on that day we remember and we say our prayers.

She's a daughter of mine. I've got three daughters, not two. Ruqiya is the eldest and will always be remembered as the eldest. She's not here, but she's still my daughter and she's part of the family. Whenever anybody asks me, 'How many daughters have you got?' I never say 'I've got two', I say, 'Three daughters. The eldest one died.'

Jane and Terry

Six years ago, Jane and Terry lost their first baby, Joshua, when Jane was twenty-seven weeks pregnant. It was discovered that Joshua had a congenital heart abnormality, and Jane and Terry were advised to end the pregnancy.

At the time of Joshua's death, they were both very shocked and distraught, and they didn't see Joshua or hold him. But some years later, they decided they would like to look at the photographs of Joshua that the hospital had kept for them. It was only then that they felt able to give Joshua his name, and grieve for him together.

Jane After Joshua was born, I felt more alone than I've ever felt in my life. Terry was trying to support me, but no one could really touch the middle of me where the pain was. I kept waiting to feel the little kicks but there was just emptiness. I thought, 'I'll never feel whole again.'

I felt I was stuck at the bottom of a black hole and the rest of the world was carrying on very fast and I'd somehow stepped off the world. Terry went back to work and things were getting back to normal and I could see that everyone was looking for signs that I was going to become 'normal' again. So I'd make an effort to behave in what they thought was a normal way, and then as soon as I was on my own, I'd lie on the floor and cry and cry. I couldn't imagine that I'd ever feel any better.

I remember when my milk came in a few days after I came home, and I was standing in a doorway with my night shirt on, and tears were pouring down my face and milk was pouring down my shirt, and I just thought, 'Is this what I've come to? I used to go out to work, I used to be able to cope with my life.' I couldn't do anything. Everything seemed immensely difficult, and not worth it. Why was I bothering, when the only important thing had gone away?

I felt very angry that for some reason someone somewhere had decided that my baby didn't deserve a life. Why my baby? Why not someone else's baby? There'd been no sign that anything like this was going to happen. I wanted to blame somebody. I felt very angry with the hospital. It didn't matter if it was their fault or not, I just had to get rid of the anger somewhere.

It helped me a lot to talk about what had happened. When I first met someone, I had to tell them almost immediately. It was as if I was testing their reaction. The loss of my baby was the most important thing about me, nothing else mattered. I told so many people. Talking about Joshua made him more real.

I needed to be on my own quite a lot. I needed space to be a wreck if I wanted to be, and I didn't want pressure to 'pull myself together'. My bed seemed a safe place. I could just be in my bed and no one was going to start asking things or expecting things of me. Sleeping helped because it blocked out the memories for a while and gave me a rest from the pain in my chest. Being so sad all the time was really physically painful. In the morning when I first woke up, I'd have a few moments feeling warm and comfortable, then I'd remember and the pain would come back. I'd think, 'Another day without my baby.'

I felt guilty about Terry because I knew that he was important to me, but I could only focus on the baby and the fact that the baby had gone. For a long time it seemed to me that Terry was dealing with it a lot better than I was. Although we talked about what had happened, it always felt as though I was the one who had suffered and Terry was the one who was trying to make me feel better. He was very sympathetic, but he seemed to have got over it in such a short time, I began to wonder whether he had any feelings about Joshua or was it only me, because I'd carried him for so long.

I didn't see Joshua when he was born and I never had an image of him in my mind. I somehow thought the hurt wouldn't be so bad or last so long if I didn't know what he looked like. After four years of trying to forget, I began to think about the photos. I felt I had to see them if I wanted to get on with my life. When I saw them, I don't know why, but I was so surprised that he looked like a baby. He became real to me then, and that's when we gave him his name. It felt like a weight had been lifted off my shoulders. I was able to say to myself, 'Yes, you did have a baby son, and it's okay to give him a name and it's okay to remember him as a part of your family and not as something that went wrong.'

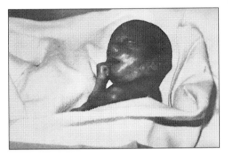

I remember when I started to smile at things again, and started to laugh. To begin with, that was very hard. Every time I laughed I immediately stopped because I felt I was betraying the memory of my baby. But gradually I had periods when I wasn't remembering all the time. There'd be times in the day when I could think about other things. Then it would come back in a great wash over me and I'd think, 'God, I forgot him. How could I do that? How could I possibly do that?' But gradually the periods got longer and I didn't feel quite so guilty about it. I began to be able to rationalise the fact that life was going to go on, and that I had to move forward, and moving forward didn't mean I was forgetting him. Somehow I had to find a way of putting his memory and the experience into a place in my life where I'd be comfortable with it. But it took a long time for those feelings to come.

When I think about Joshua now, I don't feel sad any more. It was a very, very painful experience, losing him, but he has his place now as my firstborn son. I

remember him now as a baby, a baby that's not with us any more, a very tiny baby, and somebody who is very precious.

Terry I went back to work quite quickly. In many ways that made it easy for me because I went straight back into an environment I was comfortable with and which had nothing to do with Joshua's birth and death. It meant I could hide, and I could pretend life was normal. It was only when I went back home that I was faced with the situation we were in.

People at work were very sympathetic to start with but didn't really understand and didn't want to understand. It was 'We're very sorry to hear . . .' and then 'Now let's get on.' So that encouraged me to try to forget and get on with life.

Coming home to Jane after work was difficult. I didn't know what I was going to find. She'd appear sort of normal but then she could swing very quickly into being upset and crying, and I didn't know how to handle it. I felt very helpless. I wanted to help but there didn't seem anything I could do. I tried to comfort her. I got the message very quickly that she didn't want any physical contact, and I didn't have a problem with that at all. I just did what I could to comfort her, and tried to be someone for her to lean on, but I didn't really know what to do.

People expected me to take on a typically male role. In their eyes, it was Jane who had the 'problem', and I was there to help her get better, deal with day to day things, and not necessarily to feel anything. I was supposed to get through things and get back to work. I think it's unfortunate, because it doesn't give you space to think about yourself. I used to cry over Joshua in the first weeks after his death, but never in sight of anybody. Always by myself.

Right from the start, I felt I had to be strong, and the way I showed myself to Jane had to be strong, organising everything that was happening around us. But there was a big problem with that, which I found out later on, which was that Jane wanted me to show something, which I didn't think was the right thing to do, and that led to problems between us as time went by.

What I really wanted to do was look after Jane and be the person she could rely on. So I purposely didn't show my feelings to her. I felt she needed space for her own feelings and not to have to worry about mine. I would perhaps go somewhere else and sit and think about it but not show anything to her. But because I wasn't showing anything, Jane just believed I didn't have any feelings at all and that I didn't care.

My feelings came out a long, long time afterwards. I blocked them out early on and I think it's easy for a man to do that. It wasn't until years later that by sitting down and talking, my feelings came out. I felt then I could recognise that we had had a son, and that it wasn't an event to be forgotten.

It took me a long time to realise how much I love him.

Jane and Adrian

Jane and Adrian's son Rikki was born prematurely three years ago. For some time there was hope that he'd survive. He lived for eighty-one days on a ventilator - but then he died, without ever having come home from hospital.

For Adrian, Rikki's death has been especially hard because he and Jane won't be able to have any more children. Jane has two daughters by her first marriage, but Rikki was Adrian's first and only child.

Jane Rikki was my first baby with Adrian, and Adrian desperately wanted to have a little boy. I've got two girls by my first marriage, but Adrian hasn't got any children and I feel that I've let Adrian down. I actually said to Adrian that if he wanted to leave me and find somebody else who could have his children, then I would understand. Luckily, he didn't take me up on that but I said it knowing how much he wanted to be a father. He's so good with the girls, he deserves to have children of his own.

I felt absolutely useless. Something that women all over the world can do normally and naturally, I couldn't manage. My body seemed incapable of doing something that nature had intended it to do.

I lost an awful lot of weight. I couldn't eat, I was very, very thin, and I said to Adrian, 'You can't possibly love me any more, look at the state of me.' I think I was trying to test him. Because I couldn't have a baby for him, I had to test his love for me.

But we're very lucky. We have a close, strong relationship. Somehow if one of us was down, the other managed to cope. We helped each other, we talked, we cried together. I think it's brought us a lot closer. It puts things into perspective. When you lose a baby, other things that seemed important aren't important any more. We're very, very close now. There was a time when we did shout at each other, but it was just a way of letting the anger out. We were both aware that that's what we were doing. We were able to help each other through.

I felt I would never be able to live a normal life again. I would never be able to face anybody. My instinct was to go to bed and stay there. I didn't want to get up, I didn't want to see anybody. I really felt life wasn't worth living any more.

I felt Rikki needed me with him. He was only a baby and I felt I should have been with him. I felt I had no right to live when my baby had died. I considered taking an overdose, but luckily, Adrian stopped me, because of the girls, because of him. They needed me just as much as Rikki.

I found the longing to cuddle him got stronger the more time went on. People said it would fade with time but it didn't, it got stronger and stronger.

I felt guilty that it was my fault that he'd died because I'd been incapable of carrying him properly. A couple of days after he died, someone made me laugh and I felt guilty that I could laugh after my baby had died. It didn't seem right. And I felt guilty that I wasn't with him.

I felt angry, very angry, that my baby had been taken away from me. I was furious that that could happen to my baby. And jealous that other people could have five or six children without even really wanting that many, and when I tried to have my third, I couldn't have him.

I had one friend (who at the time wasn't a friend but someone I knew) who came and sat with me. She didn't try to comfort me, she just sat and listened to me while I shouted and screamed and swore. Other people would avoid me, others would say, with the best intentions, something that would hurt. One lady said to me, 'It's probably for the best that he died', and I got very, very upset about it. Someone else said. 'Oh, he probably had brain damage. It's just as well he's dead.' Those things can hurt so much. A lot of other people would come up and say 'Hello, Jane, how are you?' and then walk off quickly because they didn't know how to speak to me.

It's brought me a lot closer to my mum and dad. Since losing Rikki, my mum and I have got very close. I always knew she loved me but somehow there was something missing. We all as a family now show our feelings for each other. We never used to cuddle each other or kiss each other but now, whenever I see my mum or dad, I have a kiss and cuddle with them , and that's important. I need to show

people I love them and feel loved as well.

With the girls, we've felt that honesty is the best thing, and if we felt like crying while we were talking about Rikki, we cried all together. We've encouraged the girls to talk to us. Jacey at one point didn't want to come and talk to us in case she upset us but I explained to her that it's a lot better to cry together than for her to bottle up her feelings. It's better to cry with someone than on your own.

About six months after Rikki died, · there were some good days but still some really bad days. I wish someone had said to me that six months is still very early and you've got to give yourself time. After six months you can still feel bad and you still hurt.

I felt I had to do the ordinary, everyday things with the girls, but I didn't want to go out. I went back to work because I needed something to do. Otherwise I would have just sat around moping. But I really couldn't see how I could lead a normal life ever again.

Somehow I've got through it and I never thought I would. I've come out the other side. There is life after a baby dies, but it just takes time. I'd like to say to Rikki now, 'I love you, darling. I miss you. I'm looking forward to the time when we'll be together again.'

Adrian

I take a lot of pride in looking after Jane and the girls and I just felt so helpless that I couldn't do more. I know it sounds crazy but I felt I should have been able to save our son for Jane. I felt worthless. I'd always promised I'd make everything happy for her and when we lost our little boy, it felt like I'd let her down in a really big way.

In some ways as time's gone on it's got harder to handle. With Jane and the kids, I know I'll go on to have a lovely life, but although it sounds horrible in a way, my life will never be as good as I hoped it would be. Because one thing even as a youngster I dreamed of was bringing up a son of my own. And I know I'm going to go on to have a lovely life with the little family I've got now, but it'll never be quite as good as I wanted because I'll never have my son with me.

I've got friends with boys getting to the age of eight and nine now and they're getting into things like football and cubs, where you always tend to see a father taking part. And I'd love nothing better than to do that sort of thing with a son of mine - whatever it was that he might want to do. And I see friends of mine with their kids and I think how lucky they are, but you have to content yourself with what you've got.

They always say it's a bad thing to bottle emotion up and I agree with that

but at the same time I don't want to put Jane through more than she's been through already. So I do bottle it up. It doesn't screw me up or anything. Perhaps with some people it would. Sometimes I get really down, but then I always make sure I'm on my own and I've got my own space. Jane says I should talk to her if I get down, but it wouldn't feel right. I just hide myself away. I don't cry very often, but I get depressed and I just tend to sit and think about him. I won't look at his photos because I still find it too hard to look at Rikki's photos, even if I'm by myself.

I used to talk to my best friend and he was quite sympathetic but I feel he's got a life of his own and he's got a young child now and he's full of it. He's a good friend so perhaps he feels he'd like to help, but it wouldn't feel right to talk to him.

I was back at work the day after Rikki died. I find that work helps me. If I'm busy, I don't dwell on bad things. I was lucky because we had a small village shop at that time and we had some wonderful customers and they said lovely things. That sort of thing helped. What didn't

couple - when we did have blazing rows. One sticks out in my mind not long after we lost Rikki. I'm a person who'll never back down in an argument and so is our eldest girl, Jacey. And although we love one another desperately, neither of us will be the one to give in. And on this occasion, I'd say one thing, and she'd come back and say something else, and we went on like this at each other across the flat, and Jane just sat down with her head in her hands and she screamed at the top of her voice 'Stop it!' It took me so by surprise, because she really did scream, and instantly it made me feel 'What am I doing here? Why am I bickering about something so stupid?' And seeing what it did to Jane, I thought, 'What an idiot I am', and of course, you say to yourself, 'I'll never do anything like that again.'

After Rikki died, I was there if the girls needed me. If they were upset, I'd talk to them and help, but I wouldn't show my feelings to them. At the time, Jacey, the eldest, made a point of being ever so helpful, and she'd come up to me and she'd say 'You're down, I know you're down.' She's a fantastic kid like that. But I wouldn't talk to her about my hurt. We said about Jacey that there would come a time when she'd shed tears about it and that's happening now and that's good.

Now, I just feel an overwhelming feeling of pride in Rikki. Because he may not have lived long, but he certainly gave it his best shot, and in the end it was just purely bad luck that he died. I'll always love him, and always feel a pride for him.

Jacey, Jane's eldest daughter, was nine when Rikki died. Her sister Donna was six. They were both with Rikki in hospital at the time of his death, and since then they've been able to talk a lot about how they feel.

Like a lot of young children who lose a baby brother or sister, both Jacey and Donna felt guilty about Rikki's death for a while. They thought that in some way they must have been responsible.

help was people saying things like 'There must have been a reason for it.' Well, it made me want to throttle them, because there was no reason why my baby should die.

The strain that a loss puts you under seems to add years to your life. I was as tired as though I'd been working twenty weeks non-stop. I felt a terrible tense feeling inside me, almost as though I wanted to smash something up simply because I'd lost my son. Particularly when I see other people with kids, it really does rub it in. I know that's terrible, because I feel really happy for people who've got kids, but at times it really does get to me and I get so angry and I feel I need some sort of release. But I'm not the sort of person who can just go to other people and discuss my problems, and luckily enough I don't go smashing anything up. I just work it out of myself. Usually I throw myself into work.

You're always on edge, and tired all the time, and what with both of us being like that and the kids as well, it goes without saying that tempers do fray and there were a couple of times - well, more than a

Donna
The worst feeling after Rikki died was really me, because I actually felt that it was me

that made Rikki die. Because when I'd kissed him, that was when his heart beat started going.

Jacey

The worst thing was the feeling of puzzlement, thinking 'Why did Rikki die?' I felt at first it must have been my fault, because if there wasn't any other reason why he died, then it must have been me. I thought I must have done something bad in my life and this was God's way of punishing me. It sounds stupid now but I believed it, and I was so scared that it was my fault.

After Rikki died, Mum was always crying. She cried so much, and I wanted to cry sometimes too, but I knew I had to be brave and I had to be strong and I had to look after my mum and Adrian and

Donna. So I did. I never cried, not even at the funeral, but I felt sad inside. Now I can cry. I had a big cry last night with my mum on the settee. After I've cried, I get this feeling of relief that I've got all the pain and the hurt and the sorrow out and it's all over and I can get on with my life. Recently I've been crying a lot. I think it's because I didn't cry early on. I feel all right when I've had a good cry with my mum.

I was worried about my mum in the first place when she told me that she was pregnant but oh, I was so happy. And I

knew it was going to be a baby boy, and I loved the name, Rikki Sean, I thought that was absolutely brilliant. And I was going to teach him to climb trees and stuff. All the boys' stuff you do - play football and that. It was going to be brilliant. But when he was born prematurely, I took it for granted that he was going to come home and I didn't spend that much time with him when he was in hospital because I said to myself, 'He's going to come home and then I'll spend time with him.' But I was too late and I regret not spending time with him.

I miss not being able to hold him and cuddle him. We used to go to the hospital and wash our hands and pick him up and we used to tell him we loved him. Knowing that he's not there and I can't do that any more, it's bad. I was going to be the best big sister in the world, but he never came home.

Delia

Delia's baby Eliza was born with an abnormality of the brain that meant she couldn't live. Doctors said she would die immediately, but Eliza survived in hospital for eight days.

It's now eight years since Eliza died, and Delia still finds it hard not knowing why her baby was abnormal. For a time it seemed that she wouldn't be able to have another baby, but six years later Delia became pregnant again and now she has a baby son called Jordan.

When they said to me Eliza wasn't going to live, I felt like my heart had broken. It was as though a knife had cut my heart in two. I just couldn't believe that she wasn't going to live. The question was, why? Why did it have to happen to me? And why wasn't she stillborn? Why did she have to have wrong with her what she had? I would have preferred it if she'd have been stillborn. They told me that she would never be able to walk or talk or anything, and I knew that she was going to die, so I had to come to terms with that, but I felt it wasn't fair. Even now, I just can't understand why she had that wrong with her.

First of all I blamed Eliza's father. I felt it was his fault. Then it was my fault. Then it was both our faults. What did I do to cause it? I must have caused it . . . he must have caused it . . . There were a lot of questions. I asked the doctors if I had caused it, and they said no, there was no explanation for it. That made it harder. I wanted an answer to explain why what she had was so devastating. So far as I was concerned there must have been an answer. But they said there wasn't.

I'm not really a religious person, but I said to myself that she was too good to live on this earth and that God had taken her and He would look after her. Then a few months afterwards my grandmother died, so I said, 'Well, God's taken my grandmother to look after my baby.' And I couldn't wish for a better person to look after her.

When I felt down, I found the best thing to do was to talk about it. I talked to friends, and I had a lot of family around me and they were all supportive. My mother and father, my grandparents. It seemed like they were all going through it with me. They were very sad and shocked. We all lived close together, which helped.

One thing that really hurt me in the hospital was that I'd been told what she had wrong with her and they said that she'd be dead within hours but in actual fact she lived for eight days. I knew she was going to die, but my dad couldn't accept that and the longer she lived, the more it built up his hopes. Which hurt me, because I knew she was going to die and there was nothing I or anybody could do. My dad's only been down to the graveyard once since she's been buried. He says it hurts him too much. He remembers her birthday and sometimes he says little things about her. He talks about 'the little girl'.

I remember her on her birthday, on the day she died, at Christmas, at Easter, on special occasions . . . On those days I go down to her grave. I put flowers on her grave, I put a birthday card there on her

birthday, a Christmas card at Christmas. Eliza would have been eight now, and I've got a friend whose son is about the same age, and I look at him and I think, 'Eliza would have been like that, Eliza would have been doing that . . .'

I've got a lock of her hair, and pictures of her in hospital, and pictures of her funeral. I keep her picture out in my living room.

What helps me most of all is that my family haven't forgotten her. When I see them, they talk about her. And they do the grave with me. I've got a large family and when she was in hospital, they all came to see her, and they all came to the funeral, which was very helpful. They don't forget her birthday. No, she's never forgotten.

Brigid

Brigid and Mike's son David is now two years old. But David had a twin brother, Sean, who died early in Brigid's pregnancy. It was some time before Brigid realised how much she needed to grieve for Sean.

I went through a very severe depression just before David was one. I had to give up work. And it took some time to sort out why it was that I was so depressed. But up until that time, I'd never grieved for Sean. It was only when David was coming up to his first birthday that Sean seemed to be saying, 'You named me but you never acknowledged my birth or my death, you haven't said hello, you haven't said goodbye, you haven't spent time with me . . .' That was what I hadn't done. And I was amazed at the amount of grief I felt.

My struggle has always been the fact that David is alive but Sean is dead. And it's very difficult, because sometimes you think, 'Gosh, if I could grieve for the two of them, then . . .' Well, it's not that it would finish, but I could actually grieve. But I have the joy of David, who is a constant reminder of a very traumatic loss.

When David was born, Mike gave him a little cuddly lion as his first toy. Then, when I became very depressed and I was grieving for Sean, I thought to myself, 'It's going to be impossible, but what I would really like to have is another lion for Sean. Because there should be two, there should be twins.' I said this to Mike, and although it was a long time since Mike had found the first little lion, he went out and he managed to get another one. And he brought back this little lion and of course, I burst into tears. I sobbed my heart out. I remember Mike said to me, 'This was supposed to make you happy', and I said, 'It does, it does.' I thought, 'Isn't he ever so special to have done that?'

So now we have two little lions and they're not played with but they sit in the cabinet and they resemble our family. David himself realises they are special and

one is his and one is Sean's. They're special to our family. One little lion has a Saint Christopher on it, and the other one doesn't. The Saint Christopher is for David, because he's still living and needs to be taken care of, but nothing can touch Sean now, he's safe. That is the difference between them.

The joy and the grief will always be there. I cannot separate them. That was the hardest thing to come to terms with.

David's birthday is especially important because we do have him, we didn't lose them both. So I really have to be happy on that day. But about three or four days before, something always triggers the sadness and I cry and cry over Sean. But the day itself, it's David's. It's a day of celebration for David. Before, the loss of Sean was like a stone around my neck that was dragging me under and every time I saw twins, or I thought about twins, I would dissolve inside. Now I can celebrate the fact that there were twins.

Daffodil and Enos

Daffodil and Enos lost their first baby, a girl they called Paris, when Daffodil was eighteen weeks pregnant. This conversation was recorded two years later when Daffodil was expecting their next baby. It was an anxious and difficult time for them.

Enos I wanted to grieve like everybody else, but I felt I had to be strong so I could support Daffodil. I felt someone had to be there to see to everything, and I had to go to work.

It wasn't that I was unable to show my emotions, but if I did, I don't know how Daffodil would have felt. She needed me to be strong. But I remember one night, I got out of bed about two in the morning and went into the front room and wept. I had such a great sense of loss. I was looking forward to holding her. And realising that I was not going to be able to do that was the hardest thing.

From the moment I found out about this next baby, I shut off. I didn't want to be too happy about it, I didn't want to plan and think about it. On occasions, we argued about that, the fact that I seemed so disinterested about the whole thing. Now I'm getting used to the idea. We're just a few weeks away now, and now I can afford to think that I might be a daddy.

It's extraordinary that it has that effect on you. Just that one loss changes your entire outlook not only on your own pregnancy but on everyone else you know who might be expecting. It colours everything.

Daffodil When they told me the baby had died, I felt it was all a really bad dream. I can remember sitting in hospital thinking, 'In a moment I'll wake up.' People talk to you and it's as though they're talking to someone else. I was quite calm for the first day or so and quite normal and I thought, 'This isn't going to be as bad as I'd thought.' But a few days later, after I'd slept and woken up a few times, I realised that it was real, and then I think I made things quite difficult for everyone around me.

I felt cheated and angry that all the things that we had planned to happen wouldn't happen. I lay there thinking 'Why me?' and then I went back into all the things that had ever gone wrong for me and I thought, 'Well, what did you expect? This always happens.'

It helped me that I had to sort out the funeral. The vicar came to see me and he was really nice about it. He was more or less my age, and it was nice to speak to someone who was completely outside it but still sympathetic. Then we had the funeral and that helped too because it meant that people were acknowledging it and not just telling me to pull myself together. It acknowledged that it had actually happened and that it had come to an end. Then I could actually think about her as a person, and that she was there, for some time if not for long. It made me not so scared of dying myself because I thought, 'If she's somewhere around then maybe one day, when I die, I'll see her.'

I felt angry with Enos for not showing how he felt. Now I know that he felt bad, but at that time I just thought he didn't care. It's okay being strong, but there were times when Enos was being so strong I didn't know he was feeling anything. So I would really have a go at him until he had some reaction, good or bad, and then I would be reassured that he felt something or was feeling the same as I was. And perhaps by then we might have gone through a full-scale argument about something that was quite trivial. I think men must think that they need to be strong, but sometimes you don't want the person next to you to be strong.

It's been hard, being pregnant again, because every day you think that something's going to go wrong, no matter what anyone says. When I first knew I was pregnant, I didn't want anyone to know until I got to a certain time, and then when I did tell them, I asked most people

not to ask me about it and just to let it go by. Then when people do feel a bit more confident about asking you, they ask you, 'Is the baby moving?' and suddenly you think, 'No, it's not.' And you think, 'Now something's wrong again.' Every day that goes past, you count it. Every time I go for a scan, I'm searching the viewer for the heart beat. I'm not looking for anything else, I just want to see the heart beating.

The doctors did every possible test they could, and that's helped me calm down. And now I can definitely feel the baby moving, it's different. But again, if I go for two hours without a movement, I get worried. Each time someone says to you, 'You've got to such and such weeks so you'll be all right now', I think, 'But that's what they told me last time.' You see something on television, or you read something, that says, 'I lost my baby at such and such a date', and you think, 'I thought I'd got past that date.' So then you've got another date to get past, and another, and another. I think if you've ever

lost a baby, if you ever get pregnant again, you don't take anything for granted. You just take it week by week and day by day, and hopefully you get through.

Enos and Daffodil's son Lewis was born safe and well a month after this conversation took place.

Part 2

WAYS OF GRIEVING

Grieving is different for everyone. There is no right way to do it. No one can say to you, 'Do this, do that, and then you'll feel better.' You have to discover what's right for you, and then do it in your own way and at your own pace.

But few people have much experience of grieving, and it isn't much talked about. So how do you know what to do? How do you even begin?

This part of the book is designed to help you think about what you'd like to do to express your grief and remember your baby.

All the ideas that are written about here have come from parents themselves. But what has been helpful for someone else won't necessarily help you. It's important to think about what *you* want.

At different times, you will feel grief in different ways and you will want to do different things. What is too painful now may be possible later on.

People are often anxious about what they 'should' or 'shouldn't' do. Family and friends aren't always understanding and with the best of intentions (usually to protect you from pain), they may discourage you from doing something that you feel you would like to do. Try not to be put off. If it feels right and you

want to do it, then it will probably help you. If you meet other bereaved parents, you're likely to find that they are doing, or want to do, very similar things.

If you lost your baby some years ago and you were discouraged from grieving at the time, you may feel you need to begin grieving now and the suggestions here could help you. In the same way, if you lost your baby very early in pregnancy, you may want to grieve but find it difficult because people don't consider your loss important and don't feel you should be sad. But many of the ideas on the following pages could be just as helpful for you as for parents whose babies died later in pregnancy or after birth.

Sometimes people feel stuck in their grieving and can't move on. A long time passes and they find that whatever they do, they still feel as sad, angry or guilty as they did when their baby died. Some people begin to feel desperate, locked into their grief and unable to think of a future. Some think about suicide. If this is how you are feeling, it's important to get help. You need to find somebody understanding to talk to, such as your doctor or an organisation that offers support. For more information, see page 45.

Remembering

'I remember I bought my wife some flowers, and I bought what I think is called a posy bowl, where it's all arranged for you and you just pick it up from the florist's. And now I can't think of buying flowers without thinking I don't want to buy a posy bowl because it reminds me of Paul.'

You may feel that you remember and think about your baby all the time and it does nothing but cause you pain. But there's a kind of remembering that, although it is painful, also brings relief.

○ Remembering can be a way of acknowledging the importance of your baby and of all that happened.

○ When something terrible happens, it's often difficult to believe it. Remembering can help you slowly believe in the reality of your baby's death.

○ You may have very few memories and this makes them even more precious. When an adult dies, there is a life time of memories. When a baby dies, there may be less to remember, but each memory is treasured.

○ If your baby died many years ago, you may have spent a long time *not* remembering, or even trying to forget. Now it may be difficult to get in touch with your memories. But if you can begin to remember, you may be able to begin to grieve.

One of the simplest ways of remembering is to talk about your baby, about what happened, and about your feelings. Look at the section on 'Talking' (on page 33) for more about this. But to talk, you need someone to talk to. The ideas in this section are all things that you can do with someone else if you want to, but many you can also do on your own.

A time and a place

Perhaps the most painful thing you can do is to sit quietly and think about your baby. You may find yourself trying to avoid it -

throwing yourself into work or other activities, keeping busy, or spending a lot of time in bed asleep. People around you may even encourage you to forget. They may say things like 'It's better not to dwell on it', and 'You've got to get on with your life.' But thinking about your baby and about the way you feel is important.

In the early time after your baby's death, it may seem that your every waking thought is for your baby and that you will never be able to stop thinking about him or her. The death of your baby may seem to have taken over your life. It won't always be like this. In time, you will be able to think about other things. But you need to give time to your baby and your feelings first.

It can help to find some special time when you can concentrate fully on your thoughts and feelings. Sometimes that can free you to get on with other things, at least for a while. Think about how you can make time for your feelings of grief, and where you would like to be.

● If your baby is buried and you have a grave to go to, or there is a place where your baby's ashes are scattered, that may be the place you want to be to think about your baby.

Many parents (though not all) find

For Jan and Dave, Daniel's grave is a very important place. They had this photo taken on the day their second baby, Charlie, was christened.

themselves visiting their baby's grave very often. Sometimes friends and relatives are worried by this - they feel it's morbid and 'unhealthy'. But for you it may be a way of feeling close to your baby, and you may feel that taking flowers and tending the grave is something you can do for someone you had little or no chance to care for.

Going to the cemetery or crematorium may also help you gradually accept the reality of your baby's death. A baby's death is so often unexpected, and it can be very hard to take in that it has really happened. This is why, for many parents, grieving begins with a struggle to accept the *fact* of their baby's death.

- Your baby's room could be the place where you want to be. If you had a room prepared, with a cot and everything made ready, then going into that room will be very hard for you, but it may also be the place where you feel closest to your baby.

In time, you may need to make yourself think about the room in some other way, and you will need to face the hard task of packing away your baby's things. There's no 'right' time to do this: do it when you feel you're ready.

- You may want to think of another place to go - a place you can think of as specially your baby's place and where you can remember and think about your baby. It may be somewhere in the countryside or a park where you can sit or walk. It could be somewhere where you have felt particularly happy in the past - perhaps a place you visited during your pregnancy.

- Going back to the hospital where your baby was born and died may be important for you, although it may be a while before you can manage it. Contact the sister on the ward to arrange a time to go, and explain that it would help you to visit and perhaps to see some of the nurses who cared for you and your baby. Most hospital staff are understanding and are often pleased to see parents again and talk. Some parents have been able to sit quietly in a corner of, say, the special care baby

unit where their baby lived and died, thinking about their baby and remembering their time there. This can sometimes help to ease the painful longing to see your baby again.

"On our way to the hospital, we both separately re-lived the last time we'd made that journey. We both knew that going into the SCBU would be hard but we had to do it. We owed it to Jason. After all, that was the only home he knew.
"It was hard walking through those doors knowing Jason wasn't there. Our eyes couldn't help searching the hot nursery. His cot was gone, a few things had been moved around. It was definitely over."

Another person whom you could contact at the hospital where you and your baby were cared for is the hospital chaplain. Most hospitals have a chapel or a quiet room where you could go. This might be especially important to you if your baby's name is entered in a remembrance book there (see page 31).

- If you have young children who are not yet at school, you may have very little private, peaceful time. Think about trying to arrange some babysitting so that you can have some time for yourself.

Just after your baby's death, you may feel that the last thing you want is time away from your living children. You may feel you want to be with them all the time, and worry a great deal when they are away from you. But some time apart when they are safely cared for and you can give time to your baby could, in the end, help all of you.

- If you're back at work, or soon will be, and feel you need more time for your feelings about your baby, think about trying to arrange some time off. Some employers are understanding and will agree to you working a shorter day, or a shorter week, for a period of time. Others may not realise just how hard things are for you, but if you can find the courage to explain, it gives them the chance to help. You could also talk to your GP, who may be prepared to sign you off work.

For some people, getting back to work is an escape and helps them regain some confidence in themselves. Even so, some days may be very hard to get through. It may help if you can give some time to yourself and thinking about your baby.

• There may be particular times during the day or night when you can allow yourself to grieve, and other times when you can't. For example, if you find sleeping difficult in the early weeks after your baby's death, you could give some time in the night to feeling sad and to crying, or perhaps to writing about your baby (see page 24), rather than trying to force yourself to sleep.

A box of treasures

Not everyone has mementoes of their baby, but most parents have something. You could gather together whatever you have in a special drawer or a box.

These are some of the things that parents keep as mementoes of their baby. If your baby died early in pregnancy, or some years ago, you may not have very many of these things. But you may be able to think of other things that are specially important to you.

flowers, pressed or dried
(these might be flowers from your baby's funeral, or flowers that you were sent in hospital, or maybe just a flower that has a special meaning for you)

your hospital appointments card

letters and cards

a scan photo

print-out from a heart monitor

your baby's cot card and name bracelet

a lock of your baby's hair

hand and foot prints (many hospitals now do these for parents after their baby's death)

birth and death certificate, certificate of stillbirth, or other 'official' documents

post mortem report

photos

baby clothes or toys

your baby's name, written on a piece of paper or card

mementoes of your pregnancy (something you wore, photos, train tickets, mementoes of a holiday . . . anything that reminds you of that time)

your diary for the year

something you have written about your baby

a poem, a piece of writing or a prayer that means a lot to you

your baby's blessing or baptism card

"For years, Holly's things were stuck in the bottom of a wardrobe in a Tesco's carrier bag, but I always had it in my mind that I'd like to do something with them. We were given this box that had been in our family for forty years, and my dad re-lined it for us and mended the lock. We keep it on our dressing table. Other people like to have things out on show, but for us it's right that Holly's things are put away in this special, private place."

You may want to contact your hospital to ask for things you weren't given at the time your baby died. For example, if a blessing was said for your baby, you could ask for a blessing card. If you lost your baby early in pregnancy, you might value a letter from your consultant, confirming your pregnancy and loss. Or if one of the midwives or nurses said a prayer for your baby, you could ask them to write down the words for you.

A book of memories

Some parents make a scrapbook, putting in many of the mementoes that might go into a treasure box (such as their baby's cot card, photos, letters and cards) along with pieces of writing, newspaper cuttings from the time of their baby's birth and death, a favourite poem, and so on.

If you buy a loose leaf book to gather these things in, you can add to it over time. You can also buy see-through plastic envelopes so that you don't have to glue precious things onto a page.

Jan and Dave made a book of memories for their first son, Daniel.

"It was having the photos that set me off. We had polaroids, but a midwife warned us they might fade. So we had photos made of the polaroids. A friend did it and enlarged them and made them all look really good. So then we needed somewhere to put them. We had the cards from the hospital too, and all the cards and letters friends had sent to us. Lots of things.

"About four months after Daniel died, we put everything out on the dining room table and put them into the book. Dave and I and my mum did it together, and we looked at all the cards again and re-read everything and talked about it all.

"Once the book was made, I showed it to a lot of people. I still do. I took it in to show

the girls at work. It made it easy to talk about Daniel and I think it helped a lot of our friends and family because there was so much in the book to talk about.

"When our second son, Charlie, was born, we made a book for him too, so that they are both treated the same. And of course I've shown Daniel's book to Charlie.

"I'm very proud of the book. I like showing it to people."

Reading

After their baby's death, parents often long to read about other people who have been bereaved in a similar way. Although reading other people's stories is distressing, it can also be reassuring to know that others have been through similar extremes of experience and feeling. It can help you feel less alone. There are now a number of books available which include the stories of parents whose babies have died, and other books describe what it is like to be bereaved and to grieve. A selection is listed on page 46.

"I wanted to read as much as I could get my hands on about stillbirth and the loss of a baby. I found it helped me, because reading other people's experiences, I could relate to them. What they were feeling was what I was feeling, and that allowed me to accept my feelings as normal, instead of thinking I was cracking up. It made me feel I wasn't the only person in the world this had happened to."

Many of the organisations listed on page 45 produce newsletters and other publications. These newsletters often include stories written by parents as well as useful information and news about the organisation's activities.

Some people want to read poetry or prose about loss and sadness. No one can tell you what to read, and you may have to read widely to find the kind of writing that means something to you. But you could begin with some of the books listed on page 46. Or try looking through anthologies of prose and poetry in your local library.

Music

You may already have a special piece of music or a song that you associate with your baby, or you may want to choose something, or even write something yourself. Listening to it can help you give time to remembering your baby.

"Holly was born two weeks before Christmas, and while I was in labour, 'Silent Night' kept coming into my head. It seemed like a gift. The words are just right, because it was a very quiet, peaceful night when she was born. We were up on the top floor of the hospital and we could see all the city lights down below us, 'calm and bright', just like the hymn says.
"For the first couple of years, I couldn't hear 'Silent Night' without crying, but it's a comfort now. Our friends know it's Holly's music and say they think of her when they hear it."

Making something in memory of your baby

You might be able to make something in memory of your baby. What you create will be a memorial, and making it will give you time to think. You can put some of the love and care that you wanted to give to your baby into the making of this special object.

These are some of the things that parents have made:

a drawing or painting

a piece of embroidery or needlework

something made of wood such as a simple piece of furniture (for the house or the garden), or something for the garden (like a bird table)

a carving

a piece of pottery

"I took great care choosing a design for an embroidered birth announcement for Neil. I found it was calming to sit and try to create something beautiful. It was something positive amongst a lot of very negative feelings. Most of all, I needed to sew during the days building up to the first anniversary, because I just needed to feel I was doing something for Neil. I sewed all through the night before his anniversary, I was so determined to get it finished for that day. Now we have it framed and on the wall."

Rather than making something yourself, you may want to have something made or buy something - any object that can be special to you and kept in a special place. It could be something that obviously commemorates your baby, with his or her name inscribed on it, or something that, to a stranger, wouldn't appear to have any special meaning.

Or you could make a collection of beautiful things - sea shells, pebbles in different shapes and colours, pressed flowers, gemstones . . . anything that attracts you and you can associate with your baby.

Writing about your baby

You don't have to be good at writing to write about your baby. Nobody need see what you write unless you want them to: it can be just for you. In fact, one of the advantages of writing is that it can be completely private. You needn't even keep what you write: you can tear it up or burn it afterwards if that's what you feel like doing.

Writing can be -

- a way of pouring out your grief so that you feel less overwhelmed by it. Writing about your baby can ease the pain, at least for a time.

- a way of recording something important so that it is never forgotten. You may even be anxious that you yourself will forget some of the details of what happened, and if you get it down on paper, you may feel calmer and more secure.

- a way of telling other people about your baby. One mother, after the death of her nine-day-old son, wrote a short piece about his life and death. She sent a copy of what she'd written to members of her family and her friends, along with a copy of a special poem that she'd chosen. It helped everyone to understand.

- a way of grasping the reality of what has happened to you and of beginning to understand your feelings. When you put something into words, you have to think about it quite carefully. Writing can be a way of sorting things out in your head - and in your heart.

Write in whatever way you want to and don't bother too much at first about grammar, spelling and punctuation. If you want what you write to be perfect, then you can go over it again later and correct it. The important thing at first is to get something down on paper as easily as possible.

Think about what you would like to write. It could be -

- the story of your pregnancy.

- your baby's story.

- a poem, a song or a prayer.

- special memories that you want to put down on paper so they are never forgotten. Try beginning 'I remember...'

- a description of the way you feel. You can do this as a diary, writing a bit day by day or every now and then, whenever you feel like writing. Put down the negative feelings as well - the anger as well as the

love, the bitter and regretful feelings as well as the sad ones. Many parents who keep a diary say it helps them later, when months have passed and they are still feeling very sad, to look back to how they felt in the early weeks. Then they realise that things are changing and they are very gradually moving forwards.

- a letter to your baby, saying all the things that you would have liked to have said if you had had the chance, and describing the plans and hopes you had for his or her future.

- a letter to your older child or children, telling them about the baby brother or sister they have lost. If they are still very young, this could be something you might keep to give to them when they are older.

- a letter to your partner, saying some of the things that you want to say but find it hard to say out loud.

- a letter to your doctor or midwife or someone who has particularly helped you. You needn't send the letter unless you want to.

- your baby's story, to give to your family and friends.

- a letter to one of the support organisations listed on page 45. Many of these organisations will reply to your letter individually.

If your loss was a long time ago, or was early in your pregnancy, you may have very little information about your baby and what happened to him or her. You may feel that you have very little you could write about. But if you sit down to recall all that you possibly can, concentrating on what you *do* remember and know rather than what you don't, you may find that there is a lot you can put down.

You could also think about contacting the hospital for information. See page 43 for more about how to do this.

Jo and Jeremy

Jo and Jeremy's son Jason lived for eleven days. Not long after he died, Jo started to write about him. She began by writing just short bits, putting down memories that she wanted to recall. She left gaps where the memories were too painful.

Gradually, she began to piece together Jason's story. She cried a lot as she wrote, sitting in her garden, or sometimes in the room that would have been Jason's. She began to feel that she'd like to put in the story of her pregnancy, too, and the months of grieving after Jason's death. She continued to write, every now and then, over several months.

She knew that to complete the story she would have to write about her most painful memory - the phone call that told them that Jason was dying, and their journey to the hospital to be with him. One day, about five months after Jason's death, she sat on a bench in the garden and wrote that part of the story. Afterwards, she found that she could read what she had written and though it still distressed her, 'it wasn't the big enemy that it had been.'

Jeremy didn't read what Jo had written for some months. When he began to read, he cried for a long time. Now, four years later, they both still read the story and are able to remember every detail of Jason's life.

Jo *"There were a number of times I just felt I was going out of my mind with the grief. I would sit in the evening and I just felt so low, so depressed and so lost that I began to wonder what was left and what was next. It was suggested that it might be helpful to write something down, and I also felt it was a nice thing to do, because Jason only lived for eleven days and if I could capture all his moments by writing it down, it would be really wonderful. So I wrote a big story about him and how I felt. And it helped a lot."*

Jeremy *"Jo's parents have read it, and her sister has read it, and afterwards they could really appreciate some of the feelings that we went through. The emptiness, the sadness, the big hole in our life. Once I start reading it, I have to read it all the way through. I can't just read a chapter. I know what the end is, and half way through the book I still go to the end to see if there's a different ending. And it's still the same ending, and I can't believe that Jo and I went through what we did and survived. because in the midst of it, you don't think you're going to survive."*

Anniversaries and special days

Every year there will be anniversaries and special days when you will grieve for your baby more intensely. You may dread the approach of these days. In the first year especially, it may seem barely possible to survive them.

If you can plan to give time to yourself, to each other, and to thinking about your baby, the anniversaries may be easier for you. It is probably best to acknowledge that the day, and the days around it, will be extremely hard. But try to plan where you want to be, what you would like to do, and how you can spend the time. If the day is empty, it will be even harder for you to get through it.

Some of what you do will be remembering your baby. You might also want to think about doing something for yourself and for each other, as a tribute to your baby.

Many parents create their own rituals, not just for their baby's anniversaries but also for other special days.

As the years pass, anniversaries will become easier, and eventually some families are able to celebrate as well as grieve.

"The first couple of years, I was very sad and I just used to sit and think about her, especially in the weeks leading up to the anniversary. But now, because she was born so near Christmas, we turn it into a day of celebration. We decided to buy a little holly bush to put in the garden so we'd always have something as a memorial to Holly, something to remember her by. And on her birthday, we make it a special day and we put the Christmas tree up and we have a little party at home. Then at twenty-five to ten on that night, Brian and I have a drink, because that's the time she was born. It's usually the days leading up the anniversary that I find difficult now - the build-up to it. The actual day isn't as bad, probably because we're doing something on that day, not just thinking about the day coming up."

Memorials

A memorial is something - anything - that will make sure your baby is never forgotten. It can be public, in the way that a gravestone is public, or it can be private and known only to you and, perhaps, your family.

Some parents know that they would like to do something to commemorate their baby but it takes them a long time - even many years - to decide what they want to do. Others want to do something, and know what they want to do, almost straight away.

"I realised that I'll never write Sean's name. I'll never write a letter to him, I'll never see a birth certificate. So I wrote his name. And while a year ago I would have written it in dark colours, with clouds, and it would have been raining, today I chose very bright colours and the sun is shining through. Because to me now, Sean is a very special gift as well as a great loss. I got angry that there was nothing - there were no photographs, no funeral, no acknowledgement at all. Just writing his name is like a memorial."

Your baby's photo

Parents have very different feelings about their baby's photos. Some treasure the pictures but find them very hard to look at. Others feel strongly that their baby's picture should be on the mantelpiece or the wall, just as it would be if he or she was alive. You may find that you move from one feeling to the other.

"It was quite a while before I could bring myself to have Neil's photograph out all the time. I'd put it away, get it out, then find it too upsetting and put it away again. But now I have copies of his photo in many places around the house. The one I see most often is on the kitchen window sill, so I see it when I'm washing up.

"We had an enlargement made but we kept it in a drawer. On Neil's fifth anniversary, I decided I'd finally go out and choose a frame for it. It was upsetting, but now I'm pleased to have the photo out and remember I bought the frame on what would have been Neil's fifth birthday."

- If your baby's photo is not very clear, or not very good quality, you may be able to find an artist who can draw or paint your baby's portrait from the photo. If you don't know anyone who could do this, it is worth asking for information from the organisations that offer support to bereaved parents (listed on page 45). They sometimes have contact with artists who have done this kind of work or who are bereaved parents themselves. You could also try a local artists' shop if there is one, or an art gallery or community centre where local artists display their work.

- If you only have polaroid pictures of your baby, a photographic shop should be able to make copies for you. Polaroids tend to fade over time. Take care when you hand over your photos. It's best to explain how precious the photos are and ask what can be done to make sure they are kept safe. If you have a good camera, you may be able to take photos of the polaroids yourself.

- Make sure you keep the negatives of your photos in a safe place. You may want to have duplicates made and ask someone else in the family or a close friend to keep the duplicates at their house.

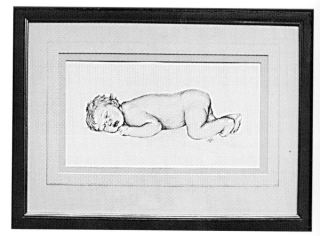

"It was Christmas morning, and there were my Christmas presents. And without me knowing about it, Phil had had these two portraits done, one of Samantha, and one of our next baby, Sophie. He'd seen an advert for babies' portraits in our local National Childbirth Trust newsletter, and he'd been to see the artist and had the portraits done for me for Christmas. The picture of Samantha is copied from the only photo we have that was taken before she died without her being attached to the ventilator and other monitors, and the drawing really captures just how she was. I couldn't believe it when I opened the parcel. It was wonderful, really wonderful."

- If you decide to frame your baby's photo, you can take time to choose the frame and make sure it is exactly what you want. Some parents are able to frame the picture themselves.

If you haven't got a photo

If you haven't got a photo of your baby, there may be some other kind of picture that you could frame and put up if you wanted to. For example -

- your baby's scan photo.

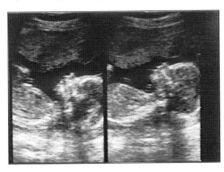

- a flower picture (see page 30) - a painting, a print, a drawing, or a picture made up of pressed flowers.

- a landscape or other scene . If there is a particular place that you associate with your baby, you could take a photo of it and have that enlarged and framed.

- a picture of something that symbolises your baby. Many parents say that they associate a particular image with their baby - a candle flame, a butterfly, waves, clouds, a bird flying across the sky, a bud opening . . .

- a piece of calligraphy. If you can't do calligraphy yourself, you may be able to find a friend or someone locally who can do it. Hospitals that have a remembrance book often use a calligrapher to make the entries and should be able to put you in touch. A beautiful piece of writing, perhaps saying no more than your baby's name and dates, or perhaps with an inscription, is something that you could frame and hang if you wished to, or just keep and treasure. If you lost your baby early in pregnancy and have no birth or death certificate, this is something you may particularly want to do.

Flowers and trees

There are many ways you can use flowers to make a memorial to your baby.

● You may want to choose one particular flower to be your baby's flower. You could choose a garden flower, or a wild flower. You can buy packets of wild flower seeds, and many have traditional meanings as well as very beautiful names. Pansies, for example, are for thoughts. Heartsease, the tiny wild pansy, is a love flower. Rosemary is for remembrance. Lilies of the valley and snowdrops are flowers of innocence and purity.

"Natasha had a little dress that had been her sister's. From a distance, the colours of it looked like the colours of a huge bunch of sweet peas. It was the nurses' favourite dress, and they used to call her 'Sweet Pea'. After she died, a friend carved her headstone for us with sweet peas growing up each side of the stone. We grow sweet peas every year and pick them to put on her grave and to have in the house."

You could look for a painting or print of your baby's flower to frame and hang on your wall.

● You might put a vase of flowers in a special place on your baby's anniversaries and other important days. Some parents buy a special vase which they keep just for their baby's flowers. If it is made of glass, or silver, you can have it engraved with your baby's name. Or you may be able to find a local pottery where they would make a special pot for you, perhaps even to your own design or in colours that you choose.

● Some parents press flowers they were given in hospital, or flowers from their baby's funeral, so that they will keep. You may want to press other flowers that have a special significance for you - flowers from your baby's first anniversary, for example. Most flowers can be pressed and you can get books on how to do it from your local library or bookshop. You could arrange the pressed flowers on paper or card and have them framed.

"Before Samantha's funeral, the sister on SCBU told us about someone local who could press flowers. So we collected a carrier bag of flowers after the funeral. We didn't have many - they were just from the family. And the lady who did the pressing talked to us about how we wanted them done, and I said I wanted them as a big picture. We got it framed, which really set it off. We have it on our bedroom wall, and I'm so pleased we've got it."

• If you have a garden, you could plant flowers in a special corner as a memorial to your baby. You could spend some time choosing different kinds of flowers to bloom at different times of the year - bulbs such as snowdrops or miniature narcissi to come up at the end of winter, primroses in the spring, forget-me-nots in April and May, daisies and little blue campanulas in June and July, pinks or marigolds in the summer. You might want to add sweet-smelling flowers and herbs, such as rosemary, lavender and thyme.

You can also grow flowers in a pot (indoors if there's enough light, or outdoors), or in a window box. If your baby is buried in an individual grave, you may want to plant flowers on the grave.

• You could plant a rose, or a flowering shrub, or a tree to commemorate your baby. If you haven't got a garden, there may be other places where, if you ask permission, you could plant something. A local school, or your hospital, might be glad to have a tree planted in the grounds. Take time to choose the shrub or tree, and to find out what kind of soil and position it needs to thrive. A garden centre should be able to give you some advice, and there will be plenty of gardening books in your local library.

If you do plant something in your garden, bear in mind that you might move away. Your bush or tree would then belong to the new owners of your house.

The Woodland Trust is a charity that exists to conserve and create areas of woodland all around the country. If you make a donation, the Trust can plant a tree, or trees, in the name of your baby and send you a certificate as a record of the planting. For more information, write to: The Woodland Trust, Autumn Park, Grantham, Lincolnshire NG31 6LL.

The Stillbirth and Neonatal Death Society (SANDS) are planning to have a rose specially cultivated for parents whose babies have died. It should be available in November 1994. You could also ask other organisations (see page 45) if they have, or are thinking of having, a special rose or other plant that you could buy.

Remembrance books

Many hospitals have remembrance books in which parents can enter their baby's name and dates and, sometimes, a short inscription. Usually these books are kept in the hospital chapel or the quiet room, and some hospitals also keep one on the special care baby unit. You can always ask to see the book first, and there will be a member of staff who can help you with your baby's entry.

"We were so pleased when the hospital chaplain asked us if we'd like Neil's name in the remembrance book. It comforts us, knowing that even though we've moved away from that place, his name is there and always will be. I'm looking forward to taking Neil's little brother to see the book when he's older and can read."

A memorial service

Memorial services for bereaved parents are sometimes organised by hospitals, and sometimes by local parent support groups, such as local groups of SANDS (the Stillbirth and Neonatal Death Society), or SATFA (Support After Termination for Abnormality). The services are usually held in the hospital chapel or a local church, and are advertised in local papers and through churches and local groups.

A memorial service can mean a great deal to parents whose babies died a long time ago and whose loss may never have been properly acknowledged:

"It's nineteen years since we lost our baby son. We didn't have a funeral. The hospital saw to everything, which we now bitterly regret. He was buried in a grave with other babies, with no headstone and nowhere we can put flowers. The whole thing was tidied away as though no one wanted to know about it.
"We read about a service for all lost babies in our local paper, and plucked up courage to go. The church was packed. It was the first time we'd met any other parents who'd suffered the same way, and it was the first

time we'd ever heard our son's name read out in public. We felt we'd come home."

Jan has helped to organise two memorial services with other parents in the local group of the Stillbirth and Neonatal Death Society (SANDS). The hospital chaplain was able to find a church where the service could be held, and they advertised it in the local free newspaper. They also had posters and leaflets printed for local post offices, GPs' surgeries, libraries and so on. When the day came, the church was full.

"As everyone arrived, they were given a candle, and during the service we lit all the candles one from another. They were all placed in front of the altar. At the end of the service, we arranged for the organist to go on playing for half an hour, so that parents could sit quietly in the church with the candles burning. We also put on tea and cakes in the church hall, so everyone could meet and talk.
"The first year we organised it, I was so on edge about it all I could hardly take part. I felt I needed another service for my baby the next day! But the second year I felt very strongly that it was a service for Daniel, and that it was his day. I think that's what all the parents felt - that it was a special service for their baby."

Jane and Adrian (who tell their story on page 10) attended a memorial service two years after their son, Rikki, died. Jane's two daughters, Jacey and Donna, went with them and it was an important occasion for them all. During the service, parents wrote their babies' names on pieces of paper and these were gathered in baskets by the children at the service. Jacey and Donna carried the baskets up to the front of the church. This is what Jane wrote about the service afterwards:

"I didn't realise so many people had lost babies. Since Rikki died, I have met quite a few people whose babies have died, yet I didn't recognise one person in that church. It was a wonderful feeling to be with so many people who truly understand the pain of losing a child. Donna and I cried all the way through the service. I personally felt it was a

tribute to my son. I had great admiration for the staff and parents who so bravely read the lessons and readings. I know I would never have managed it. I felt very proud when Jacey and Donna carried the baskets of names to the front of the church. It made the service seem more personal to Rikki because his big sisters were taking part.
"One thing I found really heart warming after the service was the way another grieving parent gave Donna a cuddle to try to comfort her. It made me feel that we are united through our losses and yet still want to help ease the pain for others."

Helping others

"I feel whatever we can do that'll help others, it's some good come out of bad."

Many parents feel that they can make some sense of their baby's death by doing something to help others. Sooner or later (and for some it isn't for some years after their baby's death), they feel that they want to contribute something, perhaps to the hospital where they were cared for, or to an organisation that works for bereaved parents or for babies. There are lots of different ways of doing this.

● Some parents join a local parents' support group, perhaps at first to get support and then later to give it. Many of the organisations listed on page 45 have local groups around the country.

"I eventually got in contact with a support group, really to go out and give some support to other people. Of course when I started talking to people I suddenly realised that I hadn't really had any support myself and I had to go through being supported, which felt quite weak. Being part of a support organisation has been important to me because it's given some more meaning to Joshua's life and death."

● You may want to raise money, for a charity or for your hospital. You could do this on your own, or with a local group. If you raise money for your hospital (for the

special care baby unit, for example), you could talk to the staff about what is most needed and raise money specifically for that. Organisations that work to support bereaved families are listed on page 45. If you contact them, they will be able to tell you what they need money for and how they could use any money that you raise.

"My baby died at a hospital where they had a lovely remembrance book and his name is now in that book. A year later we moved north, and I found out the local hospital in the town we moved to had no remembrance book. I've now raised the money to buy the book, and the hospital has agreed to pay for the inscriptions. It took me two years to do it, but when my baby died, putting his name in the book meant a lot to me and I was determined that all parents should be able to do the same if they wanted to."

● You could give a donation, no matter how large or small, to a charity, to your hospital, or to some other cause that is important or significant for you. Some families like to make a donation on their baby's birthday and think of it as the money they would have spent on a birthday present.

"The SCBU was such an important place for us and we wanted to show them how much we appreciated their care of us and our little boy. It was also important to us that we gave them something in Jason's name, something that he would be remembered by, something to mark his short life, something that would be a help to other little babies. We made a donation that enabled a monitor to be bought and a little plaque was organised for it. It meant so much to us to see that plaque, remembering Jason, our little boy."

● You may want to get involved in voluntary work that isn't connected with your grief or your baby. Think about what skills you can offer and if you don't know of any local groups or voluntary services that you would like to help, get in touch with your local Council for Voluntary Service (in your phone book, or in the yellow pages under 'Charitable and benevolent organisations').

Talking

Although some people grieve silently, most at some time want to talk about what has happened and how they feel. Talking is a way of letting out your feelings so they're not so overwhelming, and a way of understanding your feelings better so they're easier to accept. It's also a way of getting clearer in your mind what has happened to you and what it means. Saying what actually happened, and hearing yourself say it, makes it more real, and easier to believe and understand.

Talking with each other

Pat *"One of the things that helped was being able to talk about Holly. I found that if people let me talk about her, it was like having a good cry. I could release the emotions that were building up all the time. I felt I had to talk about her over and over again, going through the labour, the birth, the feelings afterwards, what we wanted for her, what should have been that didn't happen."*

Brian *"Pat would sit and she'd want to talk about it, but I couldn't. And we almost grew apart. My favourite saying at the time was 'Anyway.' As soon as she started to speak about it, I'd say 'Anyway . . .' and I'd go and make a cup of tea. I'd go out to the pub, not because I wanted to drown my sorrows, but just because I wanted to get away. I couldn't speak about it to Pat, and I couldn't speak about it to anyone else. I was bottling it all up inside myself."*

Talking together may come easily to you both. But for some couples, talking is hard.

● Try not to force it. There's no rule that says you've got to talk to each other. But try to be aware of times when talking comes naturally to you both. Often it's easier to talk when you're doing something and you don't have to look each other in the face. Try talking when you're walking together, or in the car.

● You may find it easier to talk to each other if someone else whom you both like and trust is with you - perhaps someone else in the family, or a friend who is close to you both. You could also think about going to a group together (see page 45).

● Sometimes one partner wants to talk and the other doesn't. The result can be a lot of strain and tension, and a lot of arguments. Try to recognise this situation and look for ways round it. Can the 'talking' partner find someone else to talk to? Can the 'silent' partner share thoughts and feelings in some other way - for example, by writing something down?

● Try to look for other ways of sharing your grief. When you're reading through this book, think about what you could do to remember your baby together.

"I thought it was better not to talk about it, because it only made her more upset. But I think me not talking made her feel she was carrying everything, and that I didn't care, or wasn't feeling as much as her. One day we had a blazing row and I shouted at her something like 'I loved him too, you know!' And just me saying that was enough for her, and things were a lot better after that. But it took a row to sort it out."

Grieving together

Grief can strain the closest, most loving relationship, and a lot of parents feel pulled apart rather than brought closer by their loss. When you are going through something so intense and overwhelming, it can be difficult to go on caring and thinking about each other. All your energy can seem to be taken up with your own survival: there's nothing left over for anyone else. It's also not unusual to feel angry with each other, and to find yourselves arguing at the very time when you may need each other most.

You have both lost a baby, you are both parents, and you are both bereaved. It can help to find some way to share the burden of grief, and to grieve together if you can.

● In most relationships, each partner has different strengths. But grief can upset the balance in a relationship. You may find that one of you is always supporting the other and never vice versa. After a time, this can make life difficult for both of you. The person doing the supporting can begin to feel overburdened; the person who is being supported can begin to feel put down. There can be bitterness on both sides. So try to recognise your own and each other's strengths. Each of you may be able to support the other, but in different ways or at different times.

● You may find you grieve differently and have very different feelings. This can make it hard to feel close and can cause a lot of misunderstanding and arguments. You may also find that your grieving follows a different pattern, so that when one of you is feeling low, the other is feeling rather better, and vice versa. This may make it easier for you to support each other, but it can also increase the feeling that you are isolated from each other and grieving separately.

It can help if you don't depend only on each other. Look for support outside your relationship, from others in the family or from friends. (See 'Finding someone to talk to, finding support', opposite.)

● Try to find ways of caring for each other and showing that you care. Some people don't want any physical contact with each other for some time after their baby's death. Even just hugging can seem unbearable for a time. So you may have to look for other ways of being close.

● It's not unusual to go through a time when you feel very angry with each other and want to shut each other out. This can make both of you feel very lonely. Even if you can't be close, at least try to find ways of keeping in touch. Sometimes even an argument helps. It gets things off your chest and helps you feel closer afterwards.

● If you feel your relationship is really breaking down, look for help. It's not unusual for relationships to suffer after a baby dies, and sometimes it's hard, or even impossible, to sort things out on your own. Sometimes talking to other couples, or even just having a third person (perhaps a really good friend) with you, can help. You can also contact RELATE for counselling for any kind of relationship problem (address on page 45).

Talking to family and friends

For some parents, talking to others in their family or to friends is what helps them most. You need someone whom you trust and feel comfortable with, someone who won't be shocked by anything you say, and someone who won't tell you what to do or try to make you better. Finding such a good listener isn't easy.

"My mother came down to visit me and she wanted to be with me and mother me really. But she was so upset as well that she cried, and I cried, and we didn't do anything but cry. And it didn't feel at all helpful to have somebody else pouring all that grief out with me. I felt that I could barely cope with my own grief without someone else off-loading their grief onto me as well."

People you talk to may not know how to react or what to say. They may be unable to understand your feelings, and may even say hurtful things or make you feel that you shouldn't be feeling the way you do. You may find yourself having to put on an act and pretend to be stronger and calmer than you really are.

*"Funnily enough, I found it was difficult to talk to my friends. It was as though it was too painful for them to listen to something so sad, and they would try to change the subject or make sure that we didn't get around to talking about Holly. I felt very let down and disappointed. The most hurtful thing would be when I started to talk about her to someone, a friend or a neighbour, and in the middle of it, they would cut me off or change the subject. It was worse than avoiding the subject. It was as if they didn't want to know. So as a result, when people said to me, 'How are you feeling?', instead of saying 'I feel terrible', I would say 'Fine!' And then I'd go home, slam the door, and just scream, 'No, I **don't** feel fine', and have a good cry."*

- There's a limit to the care you can give to others when you need to care for yourself and be cared for. For a time, you may have to avoid people who can't understand.

- It may help if you can be honest about what you are feeling and what you need. Often people long to help but don't know how. They want to say the right thing but don't know what it is. Sometimes you may be able to ask for what you want, or explain the way you feel and what would help.

Finding someone to talk to, finding support

You may find there's no one you can talk to, yet you may need to talk.

- Many of the organisations listed on page 45 run local support groups for bereaved parents around the country. Some also offer one-to-one befriending and telephone support. You can phone or write to find out what is available in your area. You can get in touch with these organisations, or go along to a local group without any commitment, just to find out whether it's the right thing for you.

"When I met other parents whose babies had died, I felt for the first time that I wasn't the only person in the world to have felt like this. There were other people who felt the same way and who could understand. I was able to talk about what had happened without leaving bits out and I knew that they were listening. And they didn't get fed up with hearing me, or me them."

- Think about contacting a professional such as your community midwife, health visitor or GP. Sometimes these professionals have a good understanding of bereavement and are sympathetic and supportive. Some parents find it easier to talk to someone with whom they have a less personal relationship.

- You may want to talk to your local minister or priest, or to the hospital chaplain at the hospital where your baby died.

- There may be a bereavement counsellor at the hospital where your baby died.

More and more hospitals now provide a counselling service, and this may be available to parents months or even years after the loss of their baby. It's certainly worth asking. Your GP may also be able to put you in touch with a local bereavement service or a bereavement counsellor.

You may want to think about contacting a counsellor privately. The British Association for Counselling (address on page 45) can give you details of local services. Counsellors charge between about £12 and £30 an hour, although some vary their fees according to how much you can afford, and a few offer their services free.

Counselling isn't just for people with problems or people who can't cope on their own. It helps a lot of people to talk things over in confidence with someone whose job it is to listen and who has the training and experience to understand.

"People in your family or your friends aren't always the best people to talk to. I feel we were lucky being able to speak to a counsellor. You know you're not upsetting them in the same way and you can say exactly what you feel and it doesn't matter, and you can trust them."

"When it was first suggested that we should have counselling, my immediate reaction was no, this is something we should be able to cope with by ourselves. But it was too big for us, and we did need some help."

Caring for yourself

"I didn't like my body at all after Joshua was born. Somehow, when you've had a baby that lives, you can look at your body and know it's produced something. But I just looked at my body and it looked like the picture of failure. It was saggy, with a floppy tummy, and it just looked like a complete disaster area. And I didn't want to look at it, so I just put myself in completely shapeless things, and I didn't want to do anything that would tone up my muscles again. I didn't want Terry to come anywhere near me, or touch me, or have any physical contact with me. I just wanted to shut off this piece of equipment that had failed me so miserably and never have anything to do with again."

Grieving is hard and exhausting work and it takes a lot out of you. Often it brings physical symptoms, like headaches, breathlessness, a tight feeling across your chest, and all kinds of aches and pains. Many parents speak of feeling worn out - yet they cannot rest or sleep. For women who have recently given birth, there may also be soreness and discomfort. Without the joy of a live baby to hold and care for, there can seem little reason to do any post natal exercises or help yourself recover.

Caring for yourself in physical ways can help you when you're grieving. Grief can cause tension, and exercise and relaxation can help to ease it. Grief also often brings anger, and exercise can be a way of letting some of the anger out. By exercising, you can express some of the feelings that you can't put into words. And although being kind to yourself and paying attention to your body may be very difficult to do, it can gradually help you to value yourself again.

Try to think of ways of caring for yourself.

● Exercise is important. If you have only just had your baby, you need the right sort of exercises. Do them gently and build up slowly. Most good pregnancy books include information about the exercises you need. Your community midwife or health visitor could also help you.

If it is some time since you had your baby but you haven't done any exercise since, you should still be careful. It's probably not a good idea to join the most vigorous aerobics class you can find! But there could be classes run locally that would suit you. Ask at your local library, your health centre, GP's surgery or local community or adult education centre for information.

If you'd rather not join a class, there's a wide range of books on all kinds of different ways of exercising, and also tapes and videos. With these, you can exercise in private at home.

● If you want really vigorous exercise and you're fit enough to do it, sport may be the answer.

"I was very tense, especially at work, and I found it hard to concentrate. Before Samantha died, I played football with a work team, and we used to go every Friday evening straight after work and play five-a-side. So I started playing again as soon as I went back to work about a month after Samantha died, and I found that really good and still do. I get rid of a lot of stress and anger kicking the ball about. It's good in other ways too, because the people I play with talk about Samantha and ask me how I am and how Jennie is. After Samantha died, they made a collection for SCBU."

● Exercise is relaxing, but you can help yourself relax in other ways too. A lot of parents don't want to relax. They fear that if they 'let go', their feelings will become uncontrollable and they will break down completely. It's certainly true that relaxing can bring tears, but it can also bring relief.

Try to think of what is relaxing for you. It might be something as simple as watching television, reading a good book, a soak in a hot bath, a drink, or a long walk in the fresh air. All these things are simple to do - if you can first persuade yourself that they are worth doing and that you are worth caring for.

You can also learn from relaxation techniques at classes or through books and tapes.

"Gardening helped a lot. I liked the digging, and choosing the plants, and feeling I was growing things. But I think more than that, somehow it was being in touch with the natural pattern of things - plants growing and flowering, and then fading and dying."

● Some parents are unable to sleep during the early part of their grieving. They feel too tense, too anxious, too restless and too depressed. Both exercise and relaxation could help. Taking pills is probably not a good long term answer, but if you've become very exhausted and feel unable to cope, a week's sleep with the help of some medication might be what you need. You could talk this over with your GP.

● It could help you and your partner if you can find ways of relaxing together, even if it's only slumping in front of the television together. Many couples find it hard to be close in the time just after their baby's death. Sex is comforting for some, but for others even touching each other is difficult. Look for ways of loving each other that both of you can accept.

Exercising and relaxing

1. Lie on the floor with your knees bent and your feet flat on the floor. Breathe slowly and deeply to relax.

BREATH SLOWLY AND DEEPLY TO RELAX

2. Pull your abdominal muscles in, and gradually lift your head and shoulders, pause, then lower again. Hold your arms across your abdomen if you need to support it. Repeat three times, twice a day. Remember to pull your abdominal muscles in all the time or you may damage them.

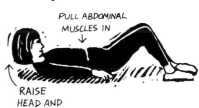

PULL ABDOMINAL MUSCLES IN

RAISE HEAD AND SHOULDERS

3. After exercising lie back, close your eyes and relax for a while.

Children and grief

All children are affected by the death of a baby brother or sister. Older, school-age children, who have some understanding of what death means, will grieve, though in a different way to you. Younger ones may not understand exactly what has happened or have any sense of loss themselves, but they will be aware of your sadness and distress, even if you try to hide it.

Children who knew their brother or sister will have different feelings to children who never even saw their baby.

● Children need to understand how you are feeling (sad, upset, angry, irritable) and why. They need to know that you loved the baby, that you are missing the baby, and that the baby won't come back. They also need to know that you also love them, and that you are not sad, upset, angry or irritable because of them.

● It helps children if you are open and honest. That includes saying, 'I don't know' when that is the honest answer to one of their questions. If children discover that they have been told something that is untrue, they become confused and can't trust you any more. Remember too that what children are not told they often make up, and what they make up is sometimes far worse than the truth.

● Children don't necessarily show how they feel immediately. It may take them a while to begin to express their feelings, and they may still be talking about the baby and about what happened some months or years later.

● Children can switch their feelings on and off. They can be sad one minute, happy the next. That doesn't mean their feelings aren't genuine or just as intense as yours.

● A lot of children feel that their brother's or sister's death must somehow have been their fault. It's hard for them to explain the death to themselves any other way. They may remember saying at some time, 'I don't want this baby', or 'I wish the baby would go away.' They need to know that thoughts like these cannot cause a baby's death. They may need a lot of reassurance about this.

It will help if you can talk about why your baby died, and if there is no known reason, explain this honestly. Sometimes children don't say how responsible and even guilty they are feeling but may become very anxious and unhappy. They need reassurance, love and security.

● Children need reassurance that they are not going to die, that you are not going to die, and that their normal, everyday life can go on. Some think that death must be 'catching' and become very fearful, especially if they get something like a cold or stomach upset.

● Children need to be able to show their feelings when they want to, talk when they feel like it, and ask questions (and get an answer) when the questions come into their heads. Talking when you think there is a need to talk doesn't usually work so well.

● Some children want to care for you as well as be cared for. Try to accept their love and support, without asking them to be 'brave' or 'grown up'.

● Many parents find it extremely hard to support and care for their children when they feel so low and in need of support themselves. Grandparents, aunts and uncles, family friends and teachers could all help.

● It's important to talk to your child's teacher. It can help if children have the chance to talk about what has happened in school, and if other children are helped to understand. There may also be times at school when your child needs someone to turn to - a close friend or a teacher.

What can help?

Doing things together. You can do a lot of the things described elsewhere in this book as a family.

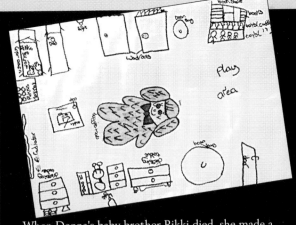

How do you look?

Draw some faces.

ANGRY   SAD   HAPPY

SCARED   GUILTY

When Donna's baby brother Rikki died, she made a special scrapbook about him. She put in drawings, a big letter 'R', some pieces of writing, photos, a prayer ... She also drew a plan of the bedroom she had hoped to share with Rikki.

"My wardrobe was going to have a high handle, and Rikki's would have a lower handle so he could open it and lots of toys would fall out. Rikki was going to have a bed near the radiator and also near the window, so he wouldn't get too hot or too cold. My bookshelf would have toys on the two bottom shelves and books higher up."

How do you feel?

Colour in the bits of your body where you feel your feelings.

sad - blue
scared - black
guilty - brown
angry - red
jealous - green
anxious - orange
happy - yellow

You could draw a picture to show what you do when you have these feelings - like shouting and stamping your foot when you're angry

Sometimes we feel sadness as aches and pains in our body. You could draw another picture and colour in those feelings.

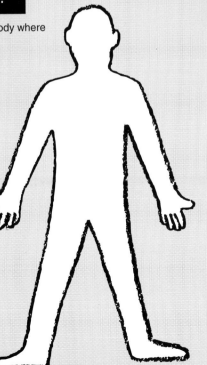

Write a story

I remember when our baby died. Our baby's name was

Write a story about your baby brother or sister who has died. Maybe you could write about how you heard that he or she had died, or what you would have liked to have done together.

39

Reading together

Some story books for children are listed on page 46. Reading together is a chance to learn about feelings without asking questions.

"My favourite memory was when he put his thumb in his mouth. It was just before he died."

The people I live with

Pretend games

MY DOLLY'S DEAD

SO'S MINE

Pretend games can help, although sometimes what children play can be upsetting for parents. You could get out some clothes to dress up in, dolls and teddies, and maybe a baby's shawl.

Draw the people in your family. You could add in your best friends, and other people. You can draw people you don't like as well as people you do.

Pets are important too.

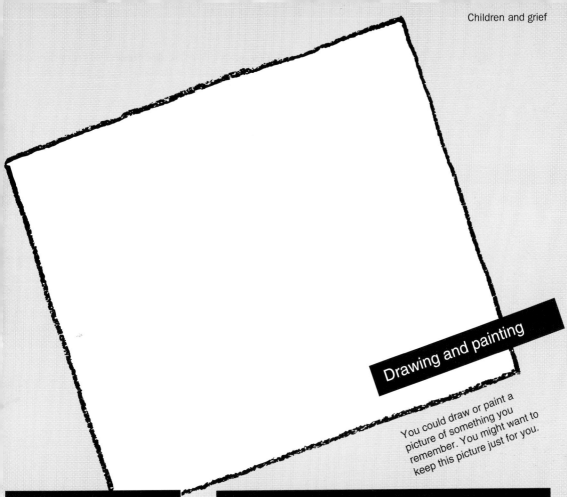

Drawing and painting

You could draw or paint a picture of something you remember. You might want to keep this picture just for you.

Saying how you feel

WHAT'S THE MATTER MUM?

NOTHING'S THE MATTER I'M FINE.

SHE'S **NOT** FINE. IS IT MY FAULT?

Showing your feelings can help children show theirs.

"Sophie's used to seeing Samantha's photos. We have photos of Samantha on our bedside cupboards, so when Sophie's in bed with us, she sees them there and points to the baby. We look at Samantha's photo album together, and as Sophie gets older, we'll talk more. I don't want Sophie to grow up in the shadow of Samantha, but I want her to grow up knowing about her big sister - and knowing how much we love them both."

Grandparents

This section is for grandparents, who may grieve not only for the grandchild they have lost but also for their child.

It is very hard to watch your child suffer, knowing that there is little you can do to help. In Pat and Brian's story (pages 2 to 6), Pat's mother says,

"I was watching Pat and Brian suffer all the time, and I couldn't do anything. I couldn't take the pain away, I couldn't give her the baby that she'd lost - my granddaughter."

Many grandparents talk about feeling helpless. They also talk about their own sorrow, which is often misunderstood and ignored. Friends and neighbours may ask you about your son or daughter, but forget that you too are grieving for the baby. If you did not have the chance to see or hold the baby, you may find it additionally hard to grieve for someone you loved but never knew.

Some grandparents also feel that the loss of their grandchild is a reminder of their own mortality:

"I had looked forward to being a grandmother ever since the children grew up, and this would have been our first grandchild. We were all excited, and it never occurred to us that anything could go wrong. When he was stillborn, and it was so unexpected, I thought, 'I'm not going to live to see my grandchildren.' "

You may have similar feelings to the parents - intense sadness, and also other feelings of anger, bitterness and guilt. You may search for a cause for the death and look for someone to blame:

"I took some of the blame myself. I felt if I'd been around more and helped more during the pregnancy, it wouldn't have happened."

"I was convinced it must have been the hospital's fault. I wanted to sue them, until my daughter gently told me that the baby was already dead when she went in."

You may even wonder whether the parents themselves may have been responsible. Sometimes it can be hard to hold back from saying, 'If only you hadn't carried on working', or 'I knew you shouldn't have gone swimming that day'.

There may be some ways you can help. If you are unsure what to do or what would be right, try to ask.

● It will help the parents if you can show them that you are sad. You may think that it will be best if you don't show your feelings, but most parents feel comforted to know that you care.

"When I went to his grave on his birthday, there was already a card there, and a small bunch of flowers, that my mum had left. She never told me that she was going to do that and I hadn't realised she'd want to. I was very touched. It changed things between us and brought us a lot closer."

● Parents often want someone to talk to. You could help just by listening. But bear in mind that often parents find it hard to talk to the people they're closest to.

● Try to find ways to acknowledge your grandchild's existence and show that he or she was important to you. Just mentioning the baby in conversation, speaking the baby's name, can mean a great deal to the parents.

If there were twins, and one lived but one died, don't be afraid to talk about the baby who died as well as the baby who lived.

● You may find yourself grieving with the parents, but make sure that your involvement is welcome. Parents can easily feel that their grief, like their baby, is being taken away from them. Or if you are very sad, they may feel that they have to look after you.

● You may be able to help in practical ways. In the time just after their baby's death, some parents are grateful to have a meal cooked or the ironing done.

- If there are older children, this may be a time when they especially need your love. They may want someone to talk to - or someone to have fun with.

> You may feel especially saddened because some years ago you yourself lost a baby. The death of your grand-child will bring back memories, and you may find yourself grieving again for your own baby. The information below may help you do this.

Parents whose babies died a long time ago

Some parents are discouraged from grieving at the time of their baby's death. Many only begin to grieve, or to grieve fully, many years later.

"Tracey died when she was five weeks and two days old. I lived on a new estate and I didn't really have any friends to talk to, and my family thought, just to protect me, that they wouldn't mention it. So I had to live with my own grief, and it was actually eighteen years later that things started to come out. I had bottled up all that grief, and eighteen years later, it was all still there."

Some ten or twenty years ago, the death of a baby (especially a baby who was stillborn) was handled very differently. Often parents did not see their baby. They were discouraged from arranging a funeral and were told to forget their loss as quickly as possible.

If this was your experience, you may now feel there's a lot you would like to do

to acknowledge your baby and your loss. Looking through this book may help you think about what would help you most. Take your time. It won't help you to rush and it's important to do what is right for you.

You may particularly long for more information about your baby. It is very hard to grieve when your memories are few and distant. And if you were deprived of information about your baby at the time of your loss, it may seem particularly important now to gather all the information you can. It is a way of acknowledging your baby's importance.

Information from the hospital

You may wish to get in touch with the hospital where you lost your baby to ask for information. Depending on the hospital, the kind of loss you had and how long ago it happened, you may be able to find out, for example, what sex your baby was, whether anything was found to be wrong with him or her, and where he or she was buried.

Some hospitals are very sympathetic and try hard to help, but others are not. There is also quite a high chance that you will be disappointed, or that you may discover something that is not as you expected and is hard to accept. One mother who badly wanted to know what the hospital had done with the body of her baby (who had died fifteen years before when she was eighteen weeks pregnant), was told that her baby's body would have been burnt in the hospital incinerator. She found this information very hurtful, although she said that it was still, for her, better to know the unpleasant truth than to know nothing at all.

If you are sure that you would like to try to find out more, the person to write to at your hospital is the Director of Midwifery Services. Unfortunately, hospital records are rarely kept for more than ten years. But if your baby died more than ten years ago, you could ask for general information about, for example, where babies were usually buried at the time your baby died.

Finding your baby's grave

If your baby was stillborn, or lived for a short time, it may be possible for you to find out where he or she was buried. For many parents, knowing their baby's burial place is extremely important. It helps them to accept the reality of something that for many years may have seemed like a dream.

If your baby was born dead before the legal age of viability*, then it is very unlikely that you will be able to find a grave. Until very recently, most hospitals have incinerated the bodies of these tiny babies, since there is no legal requirement to bury or cremate them. Fortunately, practice is now changing and many hospitals arrange respectful burial or cremation for all babies' bodies, no matter how early in pregnancy they are lost.

Think carefully before you begin to search for your baby's grave. It is not easy to do, and many weeks or months of waiting and hoping can often end in disappointment. You need to be prepared for this. You also need to know that many babies were (and some still are) buried in multiple graves along with other babies, with no gravestone to mark the burial place.

You may be able to get the help and support of a local parents' group. Some SANDS' groups (the Stillbirth and Neonatal Death Society), for example, have experience of searching for babies' graves and have good local contacts.

Your first step is to contact the offices of the cemetery in the area where your baby died. Explain what information you are looking for. You will need to give -

- your baby's surname

- your date of delivery or, for a baby who lived for a little while, your baby's date of death.

If you do not know which cemetery to go to, contact the hospital where your baby died. Write to the Hospital

* Until October 1992, the legal age of viability was 28 weeks gestation (that is, 28 weeks of pregnancy). In October 1992, this was lowered to 24 weeks.

Administrator, who will need to know -

- - the mother's full name and address at the time of the baby's birth and death

- the date of delivery.

Add any other information you may have that may help the hospital identify your baby in their records.

The hospital should be able to tell you the cemetery in which your baby is buried, or the name of the funeral directors used by the hospital at the time of your baby's death. The funeral directors should be able to tell you which cemetery was used, and you can then contact the cemetery.

It's possible especially if you live in the country, that your baby is buried in a local churchyard. You can ask for information from the vicar.

"I never thought I'd find them. I thought that something awful may have happened to them, and I never in my wildest dreams thought they'd have individual graves. I lost my son Jason twenty-three years ago and I first went to his grave on his birthday, the 22nd of January. I put twenty three yellow roses on his grave. Michael died on 11th of May and he would have been eighteen this year. I took eighteen yellow roses for him. I kept one rose at home, and it's dried beautifully. They were both stillborn, and at the time I didn't name them, though I always had Jason in mind, and I always wanted a Michael. They are actually there now. I thought I'd be sad but I wasn't, I was just so pleased to have found them. Now there's somewhere I can go. I know I can't have a stone, but I can get a flower holder. It's beyond words, it's so wonderful."

Organisations that can help

The organisations listed here vary in their size and the way they are run. Some are run by professionals and others by parents. Many of them have local contacts or support groups and they all welcome contact and enquiries from parents and others.

Support for families

BLISSLINK/NIPPERS
17-21 Emerald Street, London, WC1N 3QL (0171 831 9393/8996).

For parents of babies in intensive care and special care, including bereaved parents.

FOUNDATION FOR THE STUDY OF INFANT DEATHS (FSID)
14 Halkin Street, London SW1X 7DP (0171 235 0965).

For parents whose babies have died as a result of Sudden Infant Death Syndrome (cot death or SIDS).

MISCARRIAGE ASSOCIATION
c/o Claygate Hospital, Northgate, Wakefield, West Yorkshire WF1 3JS (01924 200799 most weekday mornings with answer-phone service out of hours).

For parents who have experienced miscarriage.

MULTIPLE BIRTH FOUNDATION
Queen Charlotte's & Chelsea Hospital, Goldhawk Road, London W6 0XG (0181 740 3519/3520).

Support for parents who have lost one or more of their babies from a multiple pregnancy or at birth.

SCOTTISH COT DEATHS TRUST
c/o Royal Hospital for Sick Children, Yorkhill, Glasgow G3 8SJ (0141 357 3946).

For parents whose babies have died as a result of Sudden Infant Death Syndrome (cot death or SIDS).

STILLBIRTH & NEONATAL DEATH SOCIETY (SANDS)
28 Portland Place, London W1N 4DE (0171 436 5881).

For parents whose babies are born dead or who die shortly after birth.

SUPPORT AFTER TERMINATION FOR ABNORMALITY (SATFA)
73-75 Charlotte Street, London W1P 1LB (0171 631 0285).

For parents who have had or may have a pregnancy terminated because of their baby's abnormality.

TWINS & MULTIPLE BIRTHS ASSOCIATION (TAMBA) BEREAVEMENT SUPPORT GROUPS
P O Box 30, Little Sutton, South Wirral, L66 1TH (0151 348 0020).

For parents who have lost one or both twins, or babies from a multiple birth.

Counselling, advice and support

ACTION FOR VICTIMS OF MEDICAL ACCIDENTS (AVMA)
Bank Chambers, 1 London Road, Forest Hill, London SE23 3TP (0181 291 2793).

Information and advice for people who believe they have suffered as a result of a medical accident.

ASSOCIATION OF COMMUNITY HEALTH COUNCILS FOR ENGLAND AND WALES (ACHCEW)
30 Drayton Park, London N5 1PB (0171 609 8405)

SCOTTISH ASSOCIATION OF HEALTH COUNCILS
5 Leamington Terrace, Edinburgh, EH10 4JW (0131 229 2344)

Community Health Councils (Local Health Councils in Scotland, Health & Social Services Councils in Northern Ireland) are independent watchdogs over local health services and can support people who wish to complain about the care they or members of their family have received. For the address and telephone number of your local Community Health Council or equivalent, see your local phone book or contact the relevant association.

BRITISH ASSOCIATION FOR COUNSELLING
1 Regent Place, Rugby, Warwickshire CV21 2PJ (01788 578328/9).

Information on where to get counselling locally.

CATHOLIC MARRIAGE ADVISORY COUNCIL
Clitherow House, 1 Blythe Mews, Blythe Road, London W14 0NW (0171 371 1341).

Marriage and relationship counselling.

COMPASSIONATE FRIENDS
53 North Street, Bristol BS3 1EN (0117 9539639).

Self-help organisation of parents whose child of any age has died from any cause.

CRUSE - BEREAVEMENT CARE
Cruse House, 126 Sheen Road, Richmond, Surrey TW9 1UR (0181 940 4818).

Support and advice for bereaved people.

JEWISH BEREAVEMENT COUNSELLING SERVICE
1 Cyprus Gardens, London N3 1SP (0171 387 4300 ext 227 or 24 - hour answerphone: 081 349 0839).

Bereavement counselling.

NAFSIYAT
278 Seven Sisters Road, London N4 2HY (0171 263 4130).

Short-term counselling and psychotherapy for black and ethnic minorities.

NATIONAL ASSOCIATION OF BEREAVEMENT SERVICES
20 Norton Folgate, London E1 6DB (0171 247 1080).

Telephone counselling for bereaved people and information about other organisations that can help.

RELATE
Herbert Gray College, Little Church Street, Rugby, Warwickshire CV21 3AP (01788 573241. Or see under Relate in your local phone book).

Confidential counselling for relationship problems of any kind.

SAMARITANS
10 The Grove, Slough, Berkshire SL1 1QP (01753 532713. Or see under Samaritans in your local phone book).

24-hour confidential telephone help for people who are in despair.

WESTMINSTER PASTORAL FOUNDATION
23 Kensington Square, London W8 5HN (0171 937 6956).

Individual, group, marital and family counselling. Information on similar services in other parts of the UK.

Pregnancy, childbirth and general

ASSOCIATION FOR IMPROVEMENTS IN THE MATERNITY SERVICES (AIMS)
21 Iver Lane, Iver, Buckinghamshire SLO 9LH (01753 652781).

Advice on rights, complaints procedures and choices in maternity care.

ASSOCIATION FOR POST-NATAL ILLNESS
25 Jerdan Place, London SW6 1BE (0171 386 0868: 10 am - 2pm).

Support and advice from other mothers who have recovered from post-natal illness.

CHILD
Suite 219, Caledonian House, 98 The Centre, Feltham, Middlesex TW13 4BH (0181 893 7110).

Support and information for families with infertility problems.

ISSUE (National Fertility Association)
509 Aldridge Road, Perry Barr, Birmingham B44 8NA (0121 344 4414).

Advice and information for people with infertility and related problems.

MATERNITY ALLIANCE
15 Britannia Street, London WC1X 9JP (0171 837 1265).

Information on maternity care and rights.

Books to read

You can get most of these books through bookshops, or ask for them at your local library. Some you have to send for.

Where several editions of a book have been published, the most recent paperback version is given here.

Erica Brown, *Children, Death and Grief*, RESPECT, Purley on Thames, 1988. Available from RESPECT, 7 Elyham, Purley on Thames, Berkshire RG8 8EN.

Susan Hill, *Family*, Michael Joseph, London, 1989.

Department of Social Work, St Christopher's Hospice, *Someone Special Has Died*, London, 1989. Available from St Christopher's Hospice, 51-59 Lawrie Park Road, London SE26 6DZ.

Nancy Kohner & Alix Henley, *When a Baby Dies. The Experience of Late Miscarriage, Stillbirth and Neonatal Death*, 2nd edition, Pandora, London, 1995.

Beverley Mathias & Desmond Spiers (Eds), *A Handbook on Death and Bereavement: Helping Children Understand*, Reach Resource Centre - National Library for the Handicapped Child, Wokingham, 1992.

Chris Moulder, *Miscarriage: Women's Experiences and Needs*, 2nd edition, Pandora, London, 1995.

Earl A Grollman, *Talking About Death: A Dialogue Between Parent and Child*, Beacon Press, Boston, USA, 1991.

Ann Dent & Alison Stewart, *At A Loss*, BaillièreTindall.

Sarah Key, *Freddie: A Diary of a Cot Death*, William Heinemann, London, 1991.

Ann Couldrick, *Grief and Bereavement. Understanding Children*, Sobell Publications, Oxford, 1989.

Antonya Cooper & Valerie Harpin, *This is Our Child: How Parents Experience the Medical World*, Oxford University Press, Oxford, 1991.

Rachel Hawley, *Special Babies Special Care*. A practical guide for parents. Supported by Prudential Carers Initiative. The Child Bereavement Trust, 1 Millside, Riversdale, Bourne End, Bucks SL8 5EB.

T Wilkinson, *The Death of a Child: A Book for Families*, Julia MacRae Books, 1991. Available from Tiptree Book Services Ltd, Church Road, Tiptree, Colchester, Essex, CO5 OSR.

Marilyn Shawe (Ed), *Enduring, Sharing, Loving: For All Those Affected by the Death of a Child*, Darton, Longman & Todd, in association with The Alder Centre, London, 1992. Poems and prose written by bereaved parents, grandparents, relatives, friends, teachers and nurses. Available from The Alder Centre, Royal Liverpool Children's NHS Trust, Eaton Road, Liverpool L12 2AP.

Paula Cruttenden Haines & Lesley Harris (Eds), *Angels of the Heart*. An anthology of poetry written by parents, grandparents, brothers, sisters and friends affected by the loss of a child. Available from Paula Cruttenden Haines, 24 Rockcliffe Avenue, Bath BA2 6QP.

Books for children

Anita Harper, *Remembering Michael*, A story about a family where a baby brother dies at birth, (a book for parents and children). Available from SANDS, 28 Portland Place, London W1N 4DE.

Jem Hughes, *Will My Rabbit Go To Heaven? and Other Questions Children Ask*, Lion, Oxford, 1988.

Joy & Marv Johnson, *Where's Jess*, Centering Corp, Omaha, USA. Available from the Foundation for the Study of Infant Deaths, 35 Belgrave Square, London SW1X 8QB.

Susan Varley, *Badger's Parting Gifts*, Armada Books, London, 1985.

Nancy C Dodge, *Thumpy's Story: A Story of Love and Grief Shared*, Prairie Lark, Springfield, USA, 1985. Available from SANDS, 28 Portland Place, London W1N 4DE.

Alicia M Sims, *Am I Still a Sister?*, Big A & Co, Albuquerque, USA, 1988.

E B White, *Charlotte's Webb*, Puffin, London, 1969.

Siobhan Parkinson, *All Shining in the Spring*, The O'Brien Press Ltd, 20 Victoria Road, Rathgar, Dublin 6, Ireland.

Althea Hayton, *Lucy's Baby Brother*, Wren Publications.

Holly Keller, *Goodbye Max*, Walker Books, London, 1990.

Elizabeth Laird, *Red Sky in the Morning*, Pan, London, 1989.